Here's information about:

- How to teach your child with a minimum of discipline
- How children discover their bodies
- Understanding the nonverbal language of the very young
- The stages in learning to talk
- Playing word games with children
- What a child thinks about and how his mind works
- The role of fantasy in a child's development

Joseph Church is coauthor of the best-selling *Childhood and Adolescence*, a book that has influenced an entire generation of parents, and a professor of psychology at Brooklyn College, City University of New York. Out of his vast experience and extensive study comes this book about successful parenthood —one of life's most rewarding experiences.

Understanding Your Child from Birth to Three

A Guide to Your Child's Psychological Development

Joseph Church

A KANGAROO BOOK
PUBLISHED BY POCKET BOOKS NEW YORK

UNDERSTANDING YOUR CHILD FROM
BIRTH TO THREE

POCKET BOOK edition published April, 1976
3rd printing.....................September, 1977

This POCKET BOOK edition includes every word contained in
the original, higher-priced edition. It is printed from brand-
new plates made from completely reset, clear, easy-to-read type.
POCKET BOOK editions are published by
POCKET BOOKS,
a Simon & Schuster Division of
GULF & WESTERN CORPORATION
1230 Avenue of the Americas,
New York, N.Y. 10020.
Trademarks registered in the United States
and other countries.

ISBN: 0-671-80483-9.
Library of Congress Catalog Card Number: 72-11417.
This POCKET BOOK edition is published by arrangement with
Random House, Inc. Copyright, ©, 1973, by Joseph Church. All
rights reserved. This book, or portions thereof, may not be repro-
duced by any means without permission of the original publisher:
Random House, Inc., 201 East 50th Street, New York, N.Y. 10022.

Printed in the U.S.A.

To Amanda and Joe

ACKNOWLEDGMENTS

A book is the product of many people besides its author. The people to whom I give credit for whatever virtues this book may have are in no way accountable for any of its deficiencies. My friend and fellow author L. Joseph Stone introduced me to the field of child development and has been a reliable source of inspiration ever since; I thank him for my borrowings from our *Childhood and Adolescence*. Gardner Spungin was instrumental in initiating this project, and I am grateful to him. I am indebted to Marvin S. Eiger, M.D., and to his excellent office staff for putting me in contact with parents. I give thanks likewise to those parents who so kindly allowed themselves to be interviewed.

CONTENTS

1.   PARENTS' FEARS

Parents read books like this one primarily because they are afraid. From the firing line of parenthood, child rearing seems a hopelessly chaotic mess, and parents pray that the Expert Authority can give them a sense of order and perspective on the process. I hope that this book achieves this goal, but it can also serve several subsidiary purposes. It can help parents know that they are not alone, that other parents share their concerns and anxieties. It can communicate to them that most of their fears are groundless, and that the solutions to most—not all—of their legitimate fears are really quite simple. Not necessarily painless, but simple.

My central thesis is that human psychological development represents a self-fulfilling prophecy: our children become pretty much what we expect them to become, whether our expectations take the form of hopes or fears. This, of course, is an argument against a fearful approach to child rearing, which generally comes out as excessive coercion and control. Children need regulating, but far less than fearful parents imagine, and overregulation leads to conflict, which engenders further need for regulation, and so on in a vicious spiral. Hope, by contrast, is expressed as affection, and well-loved babies become ever more lovable. I know that I cannot abolish fear by simple decree. Only knowledge and understanding will do the job. Which brings us full circle to the chief purpose of this book, to tell you something about the important features of how very young children operate and develop psychologically, and how you can work with normal growth processes to help your child become the sort of person you would like him or her to be.

Even as I write these words, I can feel the resistance rising. Many parents are aghast at the thought of "shaping" a person's outlook on the world. Two images arise. One is of the still all too common notion that the parent's first duty is to "break the child's spirit," to bring this wayward, unruly creature to submission, to smash his will to resist, to beat out of him the diabolical impulses that threaten to erupt without provocation. This view follows from a radically mistaken notion of what babies are like. The second image is of a more benign Skinnerian manipulation of human robots through reinforcements into some predefined set of behaviors. Again, the basic notion is at fault. Babies are not robots. They are creatures who need to learn a vast amount, but at their own pace, at the level of facts and principles and values. They will learn, and their learning will shape their outlook on the world. The question is, Who is to do the teaching? If the parents abdicate, the world will do the job. The child is not a monster, to be humanized by force, nor is he a robot to be shaped; but neither is he an angel, born into the world trailing clouds of glory, who must be protected from corruption by the lessons of life. Parents can raise their children either blindly or in awareness of the lessons they are teaching. I strongly recommend the latter.

You should know that the psychological concerns of today's parents are a fairly recent cultural development. Until about fifty or sixty years ago, parents simply *knew* how to go about raising their offspring. Parents had fears, but these centered on the baby's physical health and survival. Even these fears were muted by a fatalistic resignation to the inevitable loss of one or two children. This was brought home to me by my own mother, who expressed dismay that my wife and I were going to have only two children. Her question was, "What are you going to do when one of them dies?" Not *if,* but *when.* It had simply never entered my head that one of my robust off-spring might die.

But while our forebears worried about their children's health, it never occurred to them to be concerned about how they might be shaping their children's personalities. One simply followed the culturally given precepts for raising children, and if the child turned out badly, it was written off as flawed biology. Like Tom Sawyer's Aunt Polly, parents sometimes reproached themselves for being overindulgent, for sparing the rod, but it would never have crossed their minds to think about how they might be influencing the child's future sexuality, or intellect, or involvement in world affairs.

It was with the coming of the psychiatrists and psychologists—from Freud and Watson to Skinner and the apostles of present-day group therapies—that ordinary parents began to reflect on their child-rearing practices and the possible psychological consequences. The initial trickle of self-doubt has grown to a deluge of anxiety, and we nowadays live in what my colleague L. J. Stone has dubbed "the age of self-conscious parenthood." As parents and parents-to-be learn more about the biology and psychology of development, self-consciousness extends to ever-earlier points in the sequence of becoming parents. Is my pregnancy going well? Have I eaten or drunk or been injected or infected with something that will deform my baby? Should I perhaps have an abortion and start all over? Should we have a baby in the first place? These are all proper questions when dealt with rationally, but when they become obsessions they betray a radical lack of self-confidence. I suspect that post-partum depression, the baby blues, is becoming ever more common, and whatever the physiological basis of the baby blues, I suspect that it is made worse by excessive self-consciousness about the parental role.

From which it might be argued that if increased knowledge has disrupted established, unselfconscious patterns of child care, maybe the spread of knowledge should be reduced rather than expanded. There are two main answers to this argument. First, the old ways didn't really work very well. They produced people with very little insight into their own workings, who lived alienated from their own motives and feelings, and who automatically blamed outside agencies (sometimes correctly, of course) when their lives went awry. They produced people who were oriented to tradition rather than to evidence, people who felt locked in by destiny instead of feeling some capacity for making their own lives. They produced, finally, too large a proportion of nuts, neurotics, psychopaths, and just plain creeps. The second answer is that the knowledge that produced self-conscious parents wasn't very good knowledge, whereas today's knowledge should heighten the parent's awareness without crippling his or her ability to act. This is not to imply that all the answers are in. Far from it. We have, though, come a long way.

Freud was a great man and a revolutionary thinker, but, as it has turned out, neither he nor his followers have had much to say that is of practical use to parents. Watson was wrong in his assumption that all of development was the forming of conditioned associations into habits of action, and he was also so involved in emotional tangles of his own that many of his teachings sound like delayed strictures against his own parents. For instance, he seemed determined to eliminate feelings from child rearing—a goal that is not only futile but harmful. Gesell taught a romantic naturalism, a spontaneous unfolding according to a set universal timetable, that today seems wholly unrealistic. Spock helped, especially in the direction of getting parents to appreciate that their baby is a person who can be a source of pleasure as well as headaches, but Spock's training was in medicine, not psychology, and much of what he has had to say about psychological development does not match the evidence. B. F. Skinner's view of human beings as "empty organisms" is preposterously and wrong-headedly wrong, but his principles of reinforcement can be extremely useful across a narrow range of applications.

It is my hope, then, to give you a picture of the baby and young child as he is viewed by open-minded developmental psychologists. If this picture makes sense to you, many of your fears should evaporate and many of the puzzles about how to cope with children should solve themselves. Nevertheless, I have tried to draw some of the lessons for you. This book is not organized around the normal flow of development. It is, rather, organized around areas of parental interest and concern. Now let us look in more detail at what parents worry about.

Fears for the Baby's Physical Well-being and Survival

The baby's physical well-being is the concern of your physician, and you should turn to him for counsel in this area. It is my purpose here to catalog some widely shared concerns of parents and to offer reassurance where I can. Most physicians are busy people, with little time to comfort anxious parents, and, besides, they may be unaware of some of the questions that gnaw at inexperienced parents.

Right after birth, parents want to know two things about their new baby: Is it a boy or a girl, and is he or she all right? The first question is straightforward and usually receives a straightforward answer (we shall see later that the answer in a few rare cases has to be "Well, no, not exactly").

The second question, though, goes deeper than the simple matter of whether the baby is healthy. It also means "Is he all there or are some pieces missing?" and "Does he have any deformities or disfigurements?" Just about every parent I have ever talked to has confessed to worrying about whether the baby was going to be "all right," and the wise obstetrician knows that he has to make explicit that the baby is intact and well formed. I

16

see by a recent publication that almost all babies have birthmarks of some severity, but that most of these disappear or become unnoticeable in the first few years. It might be desirable as a part of prenatal care to advise parents in advance about the likelihood of birthmarks and their favorable prognosis. Most parents interpret birthmarks as indicators of profound pathology, such as cancer, and find after-the-fact reassurance unconvincing. Birthmarks do not always clear up completely, and I have known adults with extensive strawberry markings on their faces, but mostly such marks fade with time, and even when they do not, they do not have to be a source of psychological disturbance.

Many obstetricians do not realize that the appearance of a normal newborn baby can come as a shock to unprepared parents. Because of the way our society is organized, many people never see a newborn until confronted with their own. They have images of a plump, pink, smiling baby, and they are convinced that their own red, wizened little lump of humanity must have something wrong with him. A few babies develop a layer of fat before birth, but most are born scrawny and unappetizing-looking. Their heads seem disproportionately big and appear to rest directly on the shoulders, without benefit of an intervening neck. The head may have been squeezed out of shape by the passage through the birth canal; this molding, as it is called, goes away in the first weeks or months. The newborn's facial features are poorly defined, and he is almost chinless. His feet are ludicrously big and are bent inward at the ankles, so that the soles stare each other in the face. Both boys and girls are likely to have enlarged breasts and swollen genitals; the breasts of both boys and girls may produce a milky substance called Witch's Milk, and a small amount of blood may flow from the girl's vulva. These manifestations are caused by hormones absorbed from the mother's blood before birth and disappear within a few days. The baby's navel is marked by a stump of umbilical cord which, over a period of a week or two, dries up and drops off. The fetus in the womb has a coat of dark, downy hair. This is usually shed before birth, but not always completely, and a certain number of newborns are fairly shaggy, sometimes with hair covering much of the forehead or extending well down the back. Through their overall dismay, parents are often charmed to discover that their newborn has papery fingernails and toenails (some mothers trim them with their teeth), and a full set of eyelashes. Unless parents know in advance how ugly newborns are likely to be, they are in danger of perceiving their own perfectly normal baby as deformed.

Unless they are prepared, parents get alarmed about the jaundice that many newborn babies develop in the first few days. Parents are terror-stricken by the newborn's erratic breathing, which sounds to them like a succession of death rattles; some parents cannot sleep because they feel a need to monitor the baby's breathing, or they wake up repeatedly to make sure he's still alive. They wonder about the way he turns bright red all over when he cries, and also about the fact that he sheds no tears. They get upset when they notice that his hands and feet sometimes have a bluish cast, and they worry because the baby takes so little at each feeding. These things are alarming because parents have not been told what to expect; more basically, they haven't been told that there is anything to expect. Professionals who work with newborns get so used to their characteristics that they forget that they themselves were once startled to learn what peculiar creatures newborn humans are.

At later ages, parents worry about whether their baby may be blind or deaf. It is now possible to diagnose gross impairments of hearing and vision shortly after birth with very simple techniques, and it seems likely that diagnostic screening will become routine. The procedures can in principle be carried out immediately after birth, but the silver nitrate solution put in the baby's eyes to protect him against infection may also cause his eyelids to puff up, and if his mother has been drugged during labor he may be sluggish for a while from the drugs he has absorbed from his mother's body. When, at about age three months, the baby begins using his hands to grasp things, the awkward way his hand bends back at the wrist, the way his thumb stays in line with the other fingers instead of forming a pincer, and the labored quality of closing his fingers around an object may all lead his parents to think that he is a spastic. Parents worry, too, about retardation, psychosis, and defects of character.

Fears About the Parents' Own Adequacy

It is often not until the baby has actually been born that it dawns on the parents that they are going to have to take him home and care for all his needs. Facing up to total responsibility often produces a panic of self-doubt. Most American babies are born in a hospital, and in most hospitals the mother gets no practice in caring for the baby except for feeding him his bottle or nursing him. She does not mix the formula, or change his diapers, or bathe him, or put him to bed. The father ordinarily has no physical contact with the baby until it is time to take him home. In consequence, many parents have a feeling that the baby belongs to the hospital rather than to them, and it seems almost unfair that they should be expected to have to look after him. They feel terribly alone.

Such feelings can be counteracted by what are called rooming-in programs, which allow the baby to stay with the mother and give her and the father a chance to practice taking care of the baby under supervision before they have to assume the full burden.

Even with the help of rooming-in and various baby-care courses, the parents may feel inadequate to the task. They may fear that they will injure the baby physically or psychologically. They fear that cries will arise that they will be unable to master. They become alarmed at their own fits of impatience and anger. Most parents, determined to be loving come what may, do not anticipate the occasional rage they inevitably feel toward a baby who demands so much. They then feel guilty, as though such rage were their own unique weakness. They likewise may be startled to find that small babies may be sexually arousing. Some parents even report that they are afraid of the baby, as though he were capable of doing them harm.

As I shall keep emphasizing, parental self-confidence is essential. The baby senses his parents' anxiety, and is frightened by it. Parents have to begin by realizing that if they are concerned about the baby's welfare, their occasional blunders will do no mischief. The baby is physically and psychologically quite resilient. Obviously, parents have to control their rage, but there is nothing wrong with feeling it. In general, only severe neglect or abuse is likely to hurt the baby, and babies have to learn to live with the parents to whom they are given. Once parents have grasped that it is they who are in charge, their self-confidence will grow. As they come to know the ways of babies better, and of this baby in particular, they will find that behavior which previously was puzzling or exasperating begins to make sense. In fact, there is a logic to the way babies act; it is not like adult logic, but it makes sense, and I hope that it will take shape for the reader in these pages.

Fears for the Baby's Psychological Well-being

I was surprised to be asked by several young parents, hesitantly but with obviously real concern, whether there is such a phenomenon as the Bad Seed. Some people seem to believe that certain individuals, from conception on, carry within them the taint of inherent evil. Such individuals, it is held, are ordained to lead lives of wickedness despite anything that is done for or to them. This notion, I must assert emphatically, is nonsense. There are wicked people in the world; some are psychopaths, some are psychotics, and some are merely obtusely self-righteous. But there is nothing in their constitution that doomed them to evil. Morality is not a biological trait; people are made more or less good or evil by the experiences they have had. Parents cannot fully control their children's development; as we shall see later, the forces molding character are quite complex. But neither can parents wholly exculpate themselves with cries of "I did everything for that child." In general, as I have said and will say again, we have to be aware of the principle of the self-fulfilling prophecy: the parent who thinks he detects signs of innate evil in the child is in a fair way of raising a monster.

Parents want to know if their child is developing normally in the domains of posture, manipulation, creeping, standing, and walking and, in an important sense, that question is outside the scope of this book because physical development has only a tenuous connection with psychological development. The child who walks early is no more likely to be bright and loving than the child who walks later. The development of the child's teeth, despite what some Experts say, has no bearing on his learning ability or social maturity. Moreover, the norms of physical development were inadequately researched in the first place, and whatever utility they may once have had dwindles steadily as children change in response to improved diet, health care, hygiene, and child-rearing methods. We know nowadays that no single set of norms is going to fit all children; every culture and subculture would have its own norms, and the proficiencies studied would diverge widely. In the final analysis, the only meaningful measure is how satisfying a child is to his parents and himself.

Parents worry about discipline. They vacillate between fears that they are spoiling their child—and so producing a monster of egoism—and fears that they are overregulating him, and turning him into a passive robot. As we shall see, it is really quite simple to distinguish between indulgence and overindulgence, and between sensible control and oppression. Parents fear that they may be starving their child's creative powers, or that they are stifling these powers by teaching conventional ideas. At the same time, they fear that their child's ventures into creativity may signify a loss of contact with reality. They wonder if his fantasies will lead to chronic lying or flower into psychosis. We shall see later that fantasy is a vital ingredient in the child's development, that learning to play with ideas is essential to mature flexibility.

Parents wonder what to make of their child's sometimes outlandish fears. Here, as in the case of the child's fantasies, parents may be afraid that the child is caving in to psychosis. They are often at a loss to know what it is that is upsetting the child, or why it should distress him as much as it does. They are afraid that the child's often irrational fears may portend a lifetime of timidity. In the next chapter I will try to make some sense of children's fears, and to indicate that the child, with emotional support from his parents, does outgrow most of his fears.

Fearing perpetual dependency, parents ask how they can get a child to stop clinging to them. As soon as the child stops clinging, of course, parents feel rejected and abandoned, and may even do a little clinging of their own. A later chapter makes the point that children need to cling at first, and that premature attempts to produce independence may backfire. Everybody at every age needs people to depend on. It takes a long while to master all the relationships in which people depend on each other, to depend on people without suffocating them, and to become someone who can be depended on in turn.

In an age of shifting sex roles, parents continue to worry about masculinity and femininity. Parents have always been concerned that their son might turn out a sissy, or their daughter a tomboy. Nowadays, they go further and torment themselves with fears that their child may grow up to be a homosexual. In spite of all that has been published on the subject in recent years, many people have not been able to shake free of the conviction that one's sexual identity is a biological given. As we shall see, sex roles are learned, and what a child becomes sexually depends to a large extent on the models to whom he is exposed. More fundamentally, a changing society needs new ways of thinking about sex roles, and the emphasis from now on should be on raising a person first, and only secondarily on cultivating masculinity or femininity. Parents likewise fear that early signs of sexual feeling, as when the child fondles his or her genitals, is a mark of depravity. Ever since Freud, we have had to come to terms with the fact that sexuality begins at birth, that there is no age of innocence, and that the task of contemporary parents is to help the child understand and manage his own sexuality.

Feeding and Weaning

Infant nutrition lies in the domain of physiology and medicine, not psychology. Your pediatrician will advice you on giving your child a sound diet. Beyond nutrition, though, the feeding process, in this society and every other that I know about, takes on psychological meaning. It is in the course of feeding the baby that many important parent-child transactions take place and relationships become established. Parents worry about whether to breast-feed the baby, about the proper time for weaning, and about the psychic implications of this or that. A great deal of emotion is spent and wasted on children who appear to be "fussy" or "finicky" eaters. In some sections of our society, even where people have bought the mesomorphic (athletic-build) ideal for adult American males and the ectomorphic (slim-bodied) ideal for adult females, there is still a feeling that plumpness in infancy and childhood is a sign of good mental health. Moreover, the fat infant advertises that the father is a good provider and the mother a loving caretaker. Mixed in, however, are remnants of the puritanical view that eating is a biological necessity, not a source of sensuality, and that the child is in danger of being corrupted by an emphasis on the enjoyment of oral experience.

All that parents have to fear, after poverty and culturally imposed dietary biases that may be harmful to children, is their own anxiety. The anxious parent, as Spock has pointed out, creates feeding problems out of nothing. Normal, healthy babies are really quite sensible judges of their own diets, of what to eat and how much. They come equipped, like other animals, with a "wisdom of the body," which is far from perfect but which helps them know what is good for them (but not what is bad for them, alas!). If, from meal to meal, parents can offer the baby a variety of nourishing, well-prepared foods of good quality, the baby does an effective job of regulating his own intake. Besides which, he can learn the enjoyment of eating. Authentic gourmets do not get fat.

Toilet Training

Freud performed a great service in making us aware that sexuality is pervasive, and that sexuality is not always genital. At the same time, however, he managed to scare the living daylights out of countless parents who seemed to hear him saying not simply that traumatic toilet training will scar the child for life but that toilet training is intrinsically tyrannical and therefore traumatic. But toilet training is necessary. Those parents who forbear to train their children are really asking for trouble. Properly timed and humanely done it holds no threat of trauma.

Talking

In the good old days when people took psychological development for granted, they didn't worry about the child's talking. They knew that in his own good time he would begin to say words, that he would talk baby talk, that if he was hard to understand there was no need for concern, since he probably had nothing much to say anyway, that he could be counted on to utter an occasional cute saying, but by and large there was no hurry, since he would probably talk their ears off once he began. In recent years, however, psychological theorists—myself among them—have begun to talk about the central importance of language in psychological functioning, and parents have begun to worry about their children's linguistic abilities and what can be done to facilitate language development. I shall talk a good deal about talking, because I think language development is a fascinating topic and I hope you will, too, but in the realm of what to do about it I offer a minimum of advice. My main counsel is, as in a number of other areas, to set a good example for your child, to provide him with a model to emulate. Of course you should talk to your child, but less to instruct him in language than to commune and communicate with him.

Peer Relations

Parents begin to worry about whether their child, from a remarkably early age, will make friends easily, what kind of friends he will make and how well he will get along with them. An unsettling number of parents want to use their children to climb socially, so that parents may be less concerned about the quality of a nursery school's program than about whose children go there. The themes of selfishness and sharing crop up time and again when talking to parents. I am often surprised that no mention is made of children's hitting, fighting, and biting, although I can assure you that a fair number of children engage in these pastimes. Children reared lovingly tend to be highly social and to make friends easily. At the same time, children can be counted on to be childish, and for the most part you have to let them work out a modus vivendi with each other, even if it involves some hitting and kicking, wounded bodies and feelings, and tears of rage or sorrow. I will have some suggestions to make about the control of physical aggression, though I have no suggestions to offer about how to get your child admitted to the school that services the children of the Glamours, Affluents, and Prestiges.

Sibling Relations

Stirred by the teachings of Freud and Adler, parents become fearful at the thought of having a second child. They are afraid the coming of the second baby may somehow wreck their relationship with the first, or that the two children, in the throes of sibling rivalry, may wreck each other. A new complication has arisen in a time of population crisis. A number of parents feel guilty about wanting a second child and wonder if they wouldn't do better to have a second child by adoption. I shall try to show that fears and guilt are groundless—provided you stop at two. Brothers and sisters do indeed display a certain amount of rivalry, but this can be controlled, and at least some of the time siblings end up fast and loving friends (they sometimes end up lovers, too, but seldom at the ages with which this book is concerned). One of the pleasures of parenthood is watching siblings form a relationship which, for all the bickering, battling, belittling, and bedlam, often goes very deep.

The Future

Nowadays, with good reason, sensitive parents worry not only about their child's individual welfare but also about the larger environment in which he or she will lead a life. Dr. Strangelove is abroad in the world, looking for excuses to push a few buttons. It is a question whether the military or the Mafia will be first to seize power and suspend the Constitution, if they haven't already done so without telling us. Unorganized crime is a more immediate threat for most parents than is the Brotherhood, and in city, suburb, and small town the predatory junkie lies in wait. Urban decay has become a catchword, but the city dwellers fleeing to the suburbs find the suburbs growing into cities, often with all the inconveniences and none of the amenities of city life. In the small towns and suburbs, boredom erodes the minds and moralities of many youngsters, and the automobile becomes the Frankenstein's monster that devours us all. Paranoia is rampant, and mostly well founded.

Obviously, this book cannot tell you how to make the world safe for children. Parents, though, have an especially acute awareness of the future. Where the world's leaders seem to be sick with an egotistical cynicism that says that mankind is not worth saving, ordinary parents want an ordinary world where their children can live in scale and harmony. I can only say that it helps combat feelings of helplessness and despair if you can find ways to get involved. Incidentally, political involvement can provide an occasional escape from the confines of parenthood.

Some General Principles

Whether you are worrying about your child's eating or his toilet training, about peer relations or discipline, there are some general rules that you may find helpful. I intend to repeat these at appropriate places later on, but it may serve a purpose to set them forth here.

First of all, remember the principle of the self-fulfilling prophecy. Babies are demanding, often perplexing creatures, but they generally turn out just fine. Don't waste your time staving off imaginary disasters. If you can have confidence in your baby's future, you can have confidence in yourself. The aim of this book is less to prescribe courses of conduct than to educate your intuitions, to give you a sense of what babies and small children are like so that you will be able to make your own judgments. Friends, neighbors, and relatives will offer you abundant advice. Try neither to accept or reject such advice blindly. Instead, test it against your feelings about your baby and what you think will be good for him. And know that his future is not preordained. There are no genes that make people boors or bores. Your loving self-confidence is what he will grow on.

Learn to understand your baby's language of behavior. Long before he can talk, your baby gives you cues for appropriate action. There is a certain amount of trial and error involved, but in a short while you should be able to guess—from his posture, movements, tone of voice, and from the way he reacts to what you do—what his needs of the moment are. You will be able to tell when he is ready to sleep, when he is hungry, when he needs company, when he is about to have a bowel movement, when he wants a particular plaything.

People have known it all along, but experimental psychology in recent years has demonstrated formally the importance of models. Children grow up to be like their parents, and parents have to do the best they can to be the kind of people they would like their children to become. Obviously, as the child gets older many other people act as models for him, but parents get their licks in first.

The followers of B.F. Skinner have shown us that reward is vastly more important than punishment as a shaper of behavior, and you will accomplish far more by rewarding those forms of behavior you find admirable than by raising a row over the child's misdeeds. Punishment used judiciously has its place, but a small one, and unless it is used wisely and with restraint it rips at the essential bonds of love and trust between parent and child. Beyond simple reward there is feedback: the child's behavior should produce sensible consequences. If the baby is to get a sense of himself as competent and the world as coherent, there has to be a meaningful relationship between what he does and what ensues. In early life this usually means appropriate responses on the part of parents to the baby's language of behavior. Later, of course, it may mean verbal responses to the baby's utterances—his namings, comments, and questions.

Parents have to learn to recognize and satisfy the baby's basic needs. Here a common misconception is likely to arise. Many parents think that satisfying a baby's needs leads to spoiling. In fact, it is just the opposite. Needs that are repeatedly and reliably met go away in favor of new and more mature needs. It is the baby whose needs are not adequately gratified who goes on demanding, sometimes insatiably. Parents, of course, have to know the difference between needs, which have to be gratified for the sake of sound psychological development, and mere "wants," which sometimes have to be denied. Needs can sometimes be at variance with wants. The baby wants to stay up forever, but parents know that he needs to be put to bed, for both his and the parents' sake, so that bedtime will not become a recurring struggle. No baby has ever been known to want an immunizing injection, but parents know they are an important part of what keeps him healthy and are prepared to immobilize him while he gets his shot.

Most parents understand the baby's physical needs very well and will do their utmost to provide him with shelter, fresh air, food, and protection against disease and injury. They are less likely to know about his psychological needs and how these change with time. In practice, most parents do a fairly good job of meeting psychological needs, but often with little awareness of what is going on. Infants need a lot of physical affection, attention, play, and talk. They also need the right kinds of playthings with which to begin to learn the skills of manipulation. They need scope to move around and explore. Toddlers need all these things, but they also need a chance to develop autonomy and new kinds of competences. They need someone to listen as they begin to talk, and to respond in the right kinds of ways. The preschool child needs increasing intellectual sustenance—knowledge and ideas and viewpoints and meanings. He needs playmates as well as playthings. He needs experiences as grist to his dramatic play. He needs raw materials to shape into real and fantastic representations. He too needs people to talk with, but at a level of sophistication well beyond that of the toddler. The preschool child needs to be introduced to books; there is every reason to think that experience —or lack of it—during the preschool years has powerful effects on reading competence.

By the preschool years, it becomes evident that much of what the child does and says is an attempt to give order and meaning to his experience. Here parents have a vital role to play. They can make sure that the child has abundant stimulation and opportunity to learn, but they must also beware of trying to force the child's intellectual development and of overwhelming him with more stimulation and information than he can cope with.

Implied here is another principle: Don't rush things. Take your time and let your baby take his time. When introducing something new, whether it be solid foods or toilet training or moving to a different house, take it easy. Do it a little bit at a time, gradually. Your child's development is a marvelous thing to witness and you should allow yourself time to savor it. Remember that not too long ago he was a one-cell organism drifting down a Fallopian tube. Tomorrow he will be graduating from high school or joining a commune. So try to live in the present a little.

The Needs of Parents

I am vividly aware that parents have needs, too. They have needs in their roles as parents. They need to escape from the boredom, fatigue, irritation, and isolation that parenthood often brings. They need psychological support and reassurance.

I know also that parents are not exclusively parents. They are both individual persons and people with other roles to play. They are husband and wife and, I hope, lovers. One or both may have jobs or even careers. They have solitary or shared hobbies. They have friends with whom they like to exchange visits. They like to play cards or go to the theater or bowl or play tennis. They like to eat out or live it up from time to time. The responsibilities of parents are onerous, and if the baby comes to dominate his parents' lives completely, it is bad for both parents and child.

Thus, I hope you will build into your lives ways not to be full-time parents. At the same time, parenthood is not all agony. Besides giving your baby attention, pay attention to him. You will begin to fathom the workings of his seemingly inscrutable mind, and you should find it fascinating. Anyway, the first time he smiles at you, your viscera will turn to jelly, and your heart may threaten to burst, and you may even feel that the heartache and headaches are worthwhile. If I may borrow a line from Benjamin Spock, "Enjoy your baby!"

31

2. CHILDREN'S FEARS

If adults could recapture how they felt when they were babies, it would be much easier for them to understand the odd-seeming behavior of infants and young children. Unfortunately, this is out of the question. Adults can recall only disconnected fragments from their early years, and the ways of children remain an enigma. This is particularly true of children's fears. Children lack some fears that adults see as self-evident: fear of cars, swimming pools, and electric outlets. At the same time, a child may shrink in terror from what seems to adults the most innocent of objects—a fireplace bellows, for instance, or a dried air bladder from a piece of seaweed. Yet children's fears—and lack of fear—do make a kind of sense. If you can grasp that sense, then your own child's fears should be less a source of concern for you. Indeed, they express the child's growing comprehension, and sometimes miscomprehension, of the world, and so give us an insight into the working of the child's mentality in general.

Try to remember that without a seasoning of fear we would all be dead or incapacitated. The long-range goal is to bring up a child who is neither fearless to the point of foolhardiness, nor so fearful as to be emotionally crippled. If you see the sense in your child's fears, then you are in a position to offer loving reassurance and, sometimes, to encourage the child to explore a feared object and find out for himself that it is harmless. This should be done gently and judiciously, however. In general, knowledge is the best antidote to unreasonable fears. Out of our accumulated experience comes a set of expectations about the world in general and particular aspects of it. But knowledge cannot be rushed. Nothing is worse than to try to force a child to "face up" to a source of fear. Instead of breeding courage, one is liable to end up breeding further fearfulness. At the extreme, such forcing can lead to an inner withdrawal behind a protective coating of numb apathy. Isolated fears in a child who generally enjoys life, who feels free to explore his surroundings and to get involved with things and people, are not anything to be concerned about. All children develop some fears, and certain fears are so common as to seem necessary—or inescapable—parts of normal development. Now let us look at some of the common fears of childhood.

The Newborn Startle Response (Moro Reflex)

Although it is hardly a fear in the usual sense, the newborn baby shows a startle response analogous to the way an adult jumps when taken by surprise. Most parents have witnessed their very young baby being startled, but a few notice the highly stereotyped pattern of the reaction. Any intense, abrupt change of stimulation—a flash of bright light, a loud noise, loss of support—can trigger the startle response. The baby flings wide his arms and legs and then hugs them back in against his body, in many cases crying all the while. After a few seconds the tension subsides. Lesser changes in the level of stimulation cause the baby to become alert, to open his eyes and scan his surroundings.

Fear of the Dark

Very young babies do not fear the dark. If anything, they shun too much light. By the age of two or three months, though, many babies show great distress when they are left in a dark room. To understand why, we have to see that the newborn baby has a poorly defined awareness of himself except when he is hungry. In good balance, he stays awake briefly and then drifts off to sleep, with little concern for his surroundings. Over a period of several months, he spends more time awake and is increasingly played with, talked to, sung to—in short, he is flooded with feelings that define for him a beginning identity. This early sense of self is highly unstable and is easily threatened with extinction. It retains its continuity only by stimulation from without.

More specifically, the baby's self-awareness seems to depend on being able to see where he is. In the dark his identity is in danger of being snuffed out. As research by Witkin and associates has shown, children rely more on vision to stay oriented in space than adults do. If a child is seated in a specially made room which can be tilted left or right, he is not likely to notice when the room, and he with it, is set out of plumb. The adult, by contrast, even though the room looks to be properly oriented, is vividly aware, thanks to cues from his own body, that he is not upright. By the same token, if the child is kept vertical while just his surroundings are tilted, he feels as though he himself is out of kilter rather than the room.

Thus, without a world to look at, the child cannot know where he is, or even *if* he is. At a still later age, of course, the child will enjoy switching the world off and on in the age-old game of peekaboo, but even so he will be able to stand the suspense for only a few seconds at a time.

There are two ways to cope with fear of the dark. One

is to let the baby, in his cradle or carriage or bassinet, fall asleep in the midst of family doings. Babies have no trouble going to sleep in either noisy or quiet surroundings. However, once he gets used to one or the other, that is what he must have. For this reason, I would recommend the second course, which is to put the baby in his regular room and leave a soft light burning, at least until he has fallen asleep. In addition, the baby may need to be soothed, as by having his back rubbed, being rocked gently, or being crooned to. There should be no rush to wean the child from his dependence on the light. Even preschool and young school-age children may need a light in the room to ensure that no monsters, bogeymen, burglars, or kidnappers are lurking about.

Fear of Strangers (Stranger Anxiety)

Toward the middle of the first year, many children (about fifty percent) show fear of unfamiliar people. This fear is manifested by screaming and turning away from the unknown person; if the baby is being held when the stranger approaches, he is likely to bury his face in the neck of the person holding him. This reaction may deeply wound grandparents and aunts and uncles, who are prepared to pour forth affection and assume they will receive it in return. They feel rejected by the baby and may suspect, however irrationally, that the baby's "hostility" has been learned from his parents. Stranger anxiety occurs in response to alien places as well as people, and one can feel the baby tense up as one carries him into settings unlike those he has known.

To deal with a particular instance of stranger anxiety is very simple. The stranger has to keep his distance and wait. For the baby has a dual reaction to the unfamiliar: fear and curiosity. If the visitor can exercise a little patience and hold back, the baby, reassured, will begin to steal glances at him. If the baby finds himself being watched, he will quickly turn away again. We have to remember that eye-to-eye contact entails potent feelings, which is why people in ordinary social congress avoid it and lovers seek it. To escape too direct a confrontation with the baby, the stranger should watch him only out of the corner of the eye. Once the baby is gazing steadily, it is permissible to look at him and smile. The baby will probably react by lowering his face and smiling and squirming shyly, but the ice will have been broken. In a matter of seconds the baby will probably be making overtures of friendship, indicating that the erstwhile stranger has now been identified as human.

One such episode does not mean that the baby has been cured of stranger anxiety. Each new person will have to make his own peace with the baby, repeatedly if there are long intervals between encounters. Sometime before age six the child will have learned to be comfortable with human diversity and a range of settings, and stranger anxiety—although not necessarily shyness or clinging—will be at an end. At that point, of course, the parents will begin teaching it to him all over again: "Don't talk to (take candy from, get in a car with) people you don't know." It is small wonder that so many of us grow up paranoid.

Other fears seem to have common roots with stranger anxiety. Babies who have been reared largely within the confines of a house or apartment are likely to show fear the first time they are introduced to wide-open spaces, as on a trip to the beach. Here again, the strangeness is compounded by the fact that the child is deprived of his accustomed orientational framework. A similar distress may appear the first time a city child is set down on a patch of grass. Adults tend to find grass attractive to the touch, but to the uninitiated baby it may seem little better than a bed of nails.

One possible component in the baby's reaction to strangers, expecially those who approach too close too fast, may be the so-called "looming effect," first studied experimentally by William Schiff. That is, the baby may see the oncoming person as a large, fast-moving object that is about to crash into him. The looming effect is produced experimentally by the rapid enlargement of a shadow on a translucent screen directly in front of the propped-up baby. The baby—at least from age two weeks onward—turns his face aside, flings up his arms as though to shield his head, and cries.

Although full-blown stranger anxiety rarely appears before age five or six months, it has its antecedents at much earlier ages in the baby's different reactions to strangers and to people he knows well. He greets familiar people with smiles and squirmings and giggles, whereas strangers are met with a solemn, searching stare. There is growing evidence that babies distinguish faces from the age of a few weeks. They can make fine perceptual discriminations right after birth.

The Meaning of Stranger Anxiety

Stranger anxiety suggests that the child's familiar world —including people and places, playthings, routines of eating and sleeping, activities, and to some extent his own body—is becoming a stable known framework in contrast to which he is able to detect strangeness. He has developed a "frame of reference." But the familiar is not just "out there" in the world; the child absorbs it into the very marrow of his bones, so that his own patterns of feeling and thinking and acting come to be modeled on what he has experienced. There is a very subtle but vitally important kind of early learning which shapes the child's understanding of time, space, some sequences of cause and effect and, eventually, language, values, personal style, and sense of identity. Later on he will have no recollection of these early experiences, but they can mold his outlook for the rest of his life. For instance, the foods we are used to come to define for us the very nature of food itself, so that other, perfectly edible but unfamiliar things are treated as non-foods. Most Americans are revolted by the idea of eating grubs or seaweed or raw octopus, but in other corners of the world these are viewed as delicacies. A lifelong vegetarian tells how he vomited when he discovered that the broth he had been enjoying contained meat stock. Our concept of human beauty is shaped by our early exposure to people, so that our choice of mates in adulthood may be dictated by our experiences in the cradle. Obviously, later experiences can modify or even supersede the effects of earlier ones, but the framework laid down in the first years of life can be tenacious indeed.

The Dual Meaning of Stranger Anxiety

Coming to know the familiar is by no means the whole story. At the same time, the baby is forming powerful emotional attachments to the narrow range of people and things with which he is familiar. The child is less likely to develop stranger anxiety when he has a diverse array of caretakers, as in the kibbutzim of Israel, but his attachments are likely to be less deep. This confronts us with a dilemma. Attachment to a narrow range of people and their ways of doing things can be seen as the foundation for later prejudice and ethnocentrism, the incomprehension of and intolerance for the ways of people from alien cultural backgrounds. On the other hand, forming early attachments to a great many people seems to diffuse emotion and weaken the bonds. My own resolution of this dilemma, with which not everybody will agree, is to cultivate close attachments to the immediate family, in the hope that this will lead to a greater capacity for strong feelings in general. One can then make sure that the child's later experience will break down his ethnocentrism and allow him to form new bonds with all kinds of people.

Reactions to Novelty

Stranger anxiety is a special case of how the baby reacts to novelty. Novelty can provoke either pleasure or terror. We might say that small doses of novelty are attractive, while objects and people and places and foodstuffs that depart very markedly from the baby's past experience frighten or repel him. However, this leaves us with the problem of defining what we mean by small and large doses. For instance, the baby may not recognize his beloved mother the first time he sees her dressed up, and made up, to go out for the evening—which may complicate leaving him with an unfamiliar sitter. One would think that the residue of shaving cream left after father has shaved would be no great change from normal, but we have a record of one five-month-old boy's dismay at seeing his father thus. In both these examples we have no way of telling whether the baby sees the parent as a completely different, alien person or as a familiar person altered in a disturbing way.

One case I know of indicates that the deformation of something familiar, rather than a change of identity, can trigger fear. An eight-month-old girl was very fond of her self-righting rolypoly doll, named Otto. One day, a visitor sought to amuse her by putting the doll on its side and setting it spinning. The little girl reacted with terrified shrieks and could be calmed only when the doll had been put out of sight in a closet. Thereafter, for a period of some two months, she would peek into the closet whenever she found the door open, as though to assure herself that Otto was not moving around in that peculiar way. On one such occasion, she pointed to the doll and grunted, and her father took it out and set it down beside her. After some tentative, cautious exploration, she was able once again to play with Otto.

Separation Anxiety

Closely related to stranger anxiety, and sometimes indistinguishable from it, is separation anxiety, the distress the baby feels when cut off from those to whom he is strongly attached. Separation anxiety is thoroughly confounded with stranger anxiety when the child has to go into the hospital or when he is left in the care of an unfamiliar sitter. Nowadays, some hospitals permit or even require a parent to stay with the child, at least for short periods of hospitalization. Except in emergencies, a new caretaker should have time to interact with the child while a parent is present, easing the transition. A certain amount of separation, sometimes accompanied by separation anxiety (on both sides), is almost inevitable, and causes no lasting harm—indeed, the years-long process of emotional weaning, of letting go, has to begin almost as soon as the attachments are firmly cemented. If, though, a key person is going to be withdrawn from the baby's life for a long time, as when a parent has to go to the hospital, it should be ensured that some other person to whom the baby is attached can serve as substitute. This is one reason that babies need to have more than one parent.

The Physiognomy of Fear

Novelty is an important component in making things frightening, but it is not the whole story. Some things seem to have fear-provoking qualities built right into their appearance. This must include the way they sound, smell, taste, feel, and move or change. The analogy here is with our perception of human faces and facial expressions and the qualities they convey. People have physiognomies to which we attach such adjectives as attractive, ugly, funny, lovable, fierce, sympathetic, cold, and so forth. But nonhuman objects have physiognomies, too. For the child, and to some extent all of us, the physiognomies of objects contain "demand qualities" which evoke both feelings and actions. Various demand qualities stimulate the child to grasp, fondle, chew, hug, pound— or fear. To put it another way, objects radiate meanings. Sometimes the meanings are clouded, which can lead to either avoidance or to exploration and manipulation to find out what the possibilities are.

Many of the child's otherwise inexplicable fears make sense when we realize that he is responding to the physiognomy of something. When we put ourselves in the child's place and try to sense how things appear to him, we can sometimes guess what qualities he is reacting to. One little girl I know was terrified by the noise of the electric floor-waxer. At the same time, though, she enjoyed the sound of the vacuum cleaner and loved to ride around on its tank. I have been told of a pair of one-year-old twins who found unfamiliar babies frightening, and of an eighteen-month-old afraid of bearded faces.

The world as perceived by the child is full of all kinds of magical potentialities. The child's thinking and perceiving are not restricted by adult considerations of what is possible or impossible. As a result, young children do not always distinguish clearly between fantasy and reality. It would not surprise the child if the dead starfish on the beach were suddenly to expand to elephant size and embrace him with its tentacles. In the same way, some exaggerated action performed in fun by an adult—such as pretending to be a gorilla or moving like a mechanical man—may throw the young child into a panic.

Fear of Doctors and Nurses

Most American babies have monthly physical check-ups in the pediatrician's office or a well-baby clinic. Each visit is likely to include an immunizing injection. (Doctors are now questioning whether they may be over-immunizing children, and the smallpox vaccination is reserved for special situations.) The monthly shot, together with the handling the baby receives, is likely to produce a developing pattern of fear. On the first couple of visits, the baby may show no distress until he gets his shot, and even then it may take him several seconds to realize that something unpleasant has happened. Thereafter, he begins to anticipate discomfort. On the next visit, he starts to cry when the doctor begins examining him; and the next time, when the doctor approaches (this is still at an age when stranger anxiety is unlikely to be a factor); the time after, when he is being undressed; next, when he is carried into the examining room; then, in the waiting room. By the time he is a year old, the baby has an uncanny sense of when he is being taken to the doctor, and may start howling as soon as he leaves the house. During his second year, the baby visits the doctor at longer intervals and gets fewer shots, and by age two he and the doctor may be fast friends.

There is little that parents can do about fear of the doctor and the people who work with him except endure. They can, of course, make things harder if they allow the baby's fear to infect them with anxiety. Many parents, unfortunately, are in awe of doctors and are vaguely ashamed of the baby's display of distress. There are things the doctor can do to make his dealings with babies less traumatic, and many pediatricians are already doing them. For instance, all the undressing and dressing, and much of the handling, of the baby can be done by the parent rather than the nurse (and it is sometimes the case that one parent does better than the other at the doctor's). The parent and undressed baby can be spared long waits in the examining room. The injection can be left to the very last, when the child is ready to leave; it can be given in a buttock, which seems to hurt less if only because the baby doesn't see it coming; and it can be followed instantaneously by a mouthful of lollipop, which seems to distract the baby quite effectively from the pain. Dentists rail against doctors who give babies candy, but a once-a-month lollipop is not likely to breed many cavities.

Handling, though, is the most important part, which is why it is best left to the parent, and, when the child is old enough, to his own active cooperation. Even non-human animals resist being forcibly manipulated, and experimental procedures, such as electrical stimulation of the brain, which are aversive when done by the experimenter, lose their disagreeable character when the animal itself is allowed to control them. Many pediatricians are hurried and harried to the breaking point, but most try humanely to temper their pace to the baby's.

On the subject of dentists, it is a good idea to start the child young, around age two, on regular visits. These serve mainly to get the child used to the dentist, his office, and his paraphernalia. The child-oriented dentist, unless there is evidence of a problem, seats the child in the chair, adjusts the chair's position a few times, pokes casually around in the child's mouth, gives him a squirt or two of air and water, and sends him untraumatized on his way.

It is interesting that many children, when taken to the barber shop for the first time, usually at about age two, are afraid of the barber. I suspect that this is because the child sees the barber, with his white coat and his cabinet of gleaming instruments, as physiognomically equivalent to the dreaded doctor, with a touch of strangeness added. One nineteen-month-old got as far as being draped in the barber's cloth before he began to howl, and was summarily dismissed from the chair. After that, he refused for several days to wear a bib at mealtime, presumably because it reminded him of the barber's cloth. His mother finally got his hair cut by holding him in her lap in the barber's chair.

Avoidance of Drop-offs

The baby has one useful built-in fear, as demonstrated by Richard Walk and Eleanor Gibson, although it does not ordinarily show itself until he is able to creep. When the baby comes to a drop-off of more than a few inches, he stops short. This behavior is interesting theoretically because it shows that the baby, at least from an early age, perceives depth. In experimental situations, the baby is protected from going over the drop-off by a sheet of heavy plate glass, so that what looks like a cliff actually isn't; for this reason, the behavior is labeled the "visual cliff effect." The effect is important practically, because it may save the baby a nasty tumble. But—and this is a very big "but"—the cliff effect does *not* mean that babies can be left alone on elevated surfaces like a bed or the top of a bathinette. The effect can work only if the baby sees the drop-off. A baby can roll off a tabletop or bed and not see the brink until it is too late. Many babies enjoy flopping backward onto a bed, and they are liable to flop with the back at the very edge.

Even more important, the visual cliff effect does not work the same for all babies. Some infants see the drop-off as attractive rather than threatening, and cannot wait to launch themselves into space—we call this the "Geronimo effect." Some babies are held back by the cliff but at the same time are frightened at being so high above terra firma, so that they struggle at cross purposes with themselves trying to get down but avoiding going over the brink. The effort to get down may win out over the effort to stay put. Before babies are a year old, they can be taught to lower themselves feet first from couches and coffee tables. One should guide the baby's body, saying something equivalent to "Piggies first," and most babies get the idea quickly.

When babies begin to creep, they soon learn to creep

up any available stairs. Once at the top, they turn around and find themselves unable to come back down. It is probably the cliff effect that deters them. Many children, before they are two, figure out for themselves how to creep downstairs feet first, with much twisting around to see how they are doing. Those who don't can easily be taught to sit at the top of the stairs and to bounce down one step at a time on their bottoms.

Fears About Intactness of Body and Self

From birth on, the baby feels things. He reacts to sights, sounds, odors, and painful stimulation, whether from outside, as in the case of pinpricks or electric shock, or from inside, as in the case of colic. But his feelings at first do not seem to be tied together into the coherent, continuing awareness of the body adults possess as the background of their consciousness. When the baby first notices and grabs his feet, he gives the impression of capturing unidentified flying objects that happen to pass through his field of view; when he bites his toes, he seems surprised —and even indignant—that it hurts. Gradually, though, bodily sensations come to be knitted into a fairly well-defined image of what size and shape he is, how his parts are arranged, what he can and cannot do, what he is up to at the moment. I mentioned earlier the important part the perceived environment plays in preserving the infant's bodily integrity. But the body, for the person who inhabits it, is never merely an assemblage of anatomy kept going by physiology; it is himself the person, the vehicle of his being and identity. Thus, while perceptual experience is important for sheer physical orientation, the body as person is also defined by social experience— both good and bad.

As we have seen, in the early stages of the developing self-image, when it is still unstable, the body is felt as highly vulnerable. Because the boundaries between self and world are poorly defined, disruptions in the outside world may be felt as disruptions of the body. A toddler may show great distress if he is offered a broken cookie, or if he himself breaks it before biting into it. Here is an account of a one-and-a-half-year-old, taken from my book *Three Babies:* "Ruth was eating a graham cracker. Accidentally, she broke it in two and got upset and yelled, 'Broken! Fix! Fix!' Natually I couldn't put it together, and Ruth was very distressed that her mother couldn't fix it. She threw the two pieces on the floor and wouldn't eat them." If one of his playthings breaks, the toddler may refuse to have anything more to do with it, even after it has been repaired.

Adults sometimes find it hard to accept that the child's experience of his own body is so closely bound up with external events. It may help to point out that adults are also subject to the same influences. We all know how contagious moods and atmospheres can be. We know about the contagiousness of yawns, which bespeaks a very intimate communion between the yawner and the one affected. Listening to a speaker with a frog in his throat, we clear our own. Such effects are known collectively as empathic reactions. Watching a movie in which the hero teeters on the brink of a precipice, we empathically move our own bodies away from the edge. We work our bodies to help the pole-vaulter over the bar. We writhe empathically when watching a fight. The body English with which we try to steer a golf ball into the cup or a pool ball into the pocket or a bowling ball toward a pin belongs to the sphere of empathy. The mother spooning food into her infant makes empathic mouth movements.

Past age two and a half the child outgrows his empathic identification with broken cookies and toys, but still is very much concerned about staying intact. His broadened intellectual scope makes him aware of a whole new host of threats, some real, if remote, and some—to the adult —imaginary. The child learns about kidnappers, robbers, bad men, ferocious animals, monsters from outer space, ghosts, demons, witches, car crashes, plane crashes, shipwrecks, disease, surgery—all of them understood in highly personal terms. The child has no trouble at all constructing fantasies in which he is burned to death, trampled by stampeding cattle, devoured by crocodiles, struck by lightning, shot at, swept away by flood or windstorm, and generally annihilated.

Notice, though, an important element that is coming into play. The child may scare himself with his imaginings, but most of the time he enjoys them. Apart from the thrill of adventure, his picturing various horrors helps the child to come to terms with them and surmount them. His knowledge of possible menaces influences his everyday behavior hardly at all: he still has to be warned against strangers, he still cannot be trusted to cross the street unescorted, matches have to be kept out of his reach, and all the rest. It almost seems that the visual cliff effect stops operating in preschool children, since all too many of them fall from high places.

There is nothing to do about the child's fears for his own intactness except to avoid making them worse. Nannies and older relatives are still prone to telling the child cautionary tales—like the one about the boy whose hand stuck out of the grave because he had slapped an adult, or about devils carrying recalcitrant children off to hell—and these can drive the child to nightmares.

The followers of Sigmund Freud relate the body fears of the preschool period to the playing out of the Oedipus complex and fears of castration. It seems simpler to say that the child's experience of self and world is inherently unstable and that instability is threatening, so that the child strives for order and stability and predictability. Sometimes, in resisting the possibility of a magical dissolution of self and world, he adopts an almost ritualistic rigidity, insisting that his clothes go on and off in a fixed order, that key playthings not be moved, that bedtime follow a standard ritual, such as singing a particular song three times, and so forth. If parents understand this, they can sympathetically encourage the child to test himself against the world—to climb one rung higher, to try putting his face in the water, to jump from the top of the jungle gym into adult arms, to let go and slide down full speed—and discover his own powers of mastery.

Fear of Death

The infant and toddler know nothing of death and so cannot be disturbed by thoughts about it. The young preschool child's first acquaintance with death is likely to take the form of seeing dead insects or animals. He accepts death casually. Asked what death is, he replies along the lines of "You put it in the garbage can." Throughout the first few years death as an abstract concept is not taken too seriously. In their games of violence preschoolers typically shout, "Bang! Bang! You're dead. Now you must be alive again."

By age three or so, however, the child becomes aware of another, more concrete and immediate form of death. This is at first a realization that the individual people close to him are mortal, that they can be taken from him —a new source of separation anxiety. His concern is not so much for those who may be stricken, but rather for himself who may be deprived. Only later, usually during the school years, does it dawn on the child that he too may die. His earlier fantasies of disaster somehow never followed through to death as a logical outcome.

The knowledge that his parents might die comes as a severe jolt to the child. He repeatedly asks, "When are you going to die, Daddy?" and "You're not going to die, are you, Mommy?" He may cling fiercely to a parent, proclaiming, "I don't want you to die! Not ever!" His later awareness of his own mortality produces further distress. The child may be reluctant to go to sleep, since to yield to unconsciousness may be the gateway to permanent oblivion.

How can parents cope with the child's fear of death? Realistically, as long as nobody is imminently moribund. The only honest thing you can say is that everybody dies sooner or later, but that the parents have no expectation of dying in the near future, they expect to be around to look after the child for as long as he needs them, and that there is no reason a sound, healthy child like yours shouldn't live a good long time. Some parents may be tempted to slip in some comments about using one's time on earth to good advantage, but these will almost certainly be lost on the child. If the child insists on knowing whether the parents fear death, honesty is called for. Most people will answer that they certainly do, but that it is not an immediate problem and therefore not to be dwelt upon unduly, and it is more important to think about how to live. Sooner or later, it may become appropriate to say that death may be preferable to the vegetable state in which some people survive.

For most children, honest dealing with the question of death is an important part of making sense of one's existence. The total process, of course, extends over a number of years, perhaps throughout life. The rules change somewhat, however, when death is not something in the far future but is close at hand. Let us consider first the case where the child himself has a fatal disease. One's first impulse is to make the child's brief stay on earth as pleasant as possible; in practice, though, this is less a matter of pouring life's riches on the child than of giving him as nearly normal a childhood as possible. He needs attention and loving and protection to exactly the same degree as well children, but he also needs regulation, discipline, and control the way normal children do. Afflicted children need as much give-and-take with their peers as their condition will allow. Childhood is most satisfying to children who have to cope with life's demands. It is unfair to the child to make a life for him based on the premise that he will not get his fair share of the world's delights. There is no surer way to convey to a child that he is "different"—the last thing young children want to be, on any dimension—than to shower him with indulgences and make him the center of the universe. This is not an easy lesson to assimilate, but parents who truly care about their child, even if he will be theirs only for a short time, have to learn it.

What does one tell a dying child about death? Exactly what one tells a healthy child—and no more. When it comes to the child's own future, to tell him that he will die soon serves absolutely no constructive purpose, and truth-telling has to be shaded in the interests of mercy. If the moribund child asks, "Am I going to die?" the answer is, "Of course, everybody has to die someday." But if, in physical misery, he asks, "Am I dying?" the answer is a lie or at least an evasion. Since children are quick to detect evasiveness, it is better to be prepared with a simple falsehood, such as, "Of course not, silly. You're very sick, but the doctor is working hard to get you all well again."

In religious families, there will be concern that the child be assured of salvation. Since, in most faiths, the child is not thought to reach the "age of reason," when he can choose to behave sinfully, until about age seven, this is not an issue for the readers of this book. Whatever religious instruction is given the child, including ideas about life after death, can be done unthreateningly, without any implication that the child himself may soon be chosen for salvation or damnation.

If it is a parent or other person close to the child who is close to death, the child has to be prepared for the event. However, the preparation should not come too far in advance. The child who is told that someone he loves is going to die soon will probably be seriously upset; but if death is months in coming, the fact will lose its reality for the child and he will then be doubly disturbed when faced with the actuality.

What with the segregation between the generations,

many children nowadays grow up without any firsthand contact with death. Even when a grandparent dies, it is likely to be a remote event without great emotional significance for the child. Parents have to be prepared to cope not only with the child's grief but with his indifference. He is not morally defective if he feels no great loss when a person dies whom he has not known very intimately. Nevertheless, a certain number of children do lose somebody they have known and loved, and the problem remains of how to help a child in these circumstances handle his feelings. Again, honesty is in order. Using euphemisms in speaking of death serves only to confuse and further frighten a child. The parents should not try to conceal their own feelings from the child. They should try to keep under control the expression of feelings, but not deny their nature. It is all very well to say that Grandpa's troubles are now over, that he is well quit of this vale of tears, that he is happy now in Heaven, but this will not mask how the parents really feel.

Equally important, parents should not try to conceal their own feelings from themselves. These are likely to be rather more complex than simple grief. They may contain strands of remorse and guilt for neglecting the person while he was alive. There may even be some small element of relief that one no longer has to think about the dead person. There may be irritation that one has to assume some of the departed's obligations. One may even be jealous over the partition of the dead person's estate. There is no reason to share all these complexities with the child. But you should not be surprised if he senses that there are other feelings at work and presses you to tell him about them.

The elaborate and often gruesome corpse worship that has become part of the American Way of Death, together with its ornate trappings, help to invest death with further mystery and terror for the child, and to distract him from the simple truth that someone he loved will not be around any more. A child will feel ambivalent about seeing the corpse. Most children are enormously curious about what a dead person looks like, but they are also in some dread about finding out. In the final analysis, the decision has to be left to the child, who should be given support in whatever he chooses. Various religious and ethnic customs may prescribe certain behavior for the child, but these are not morally binding and parents should think first of what is good for their own child.

Communicating Parental Fears to the Child

As parents, we definitely want to teach the child some reasonable and realistic fears. At the same time, we want to avoid handing on the one or more irrational fears that most of us possess—fear of thunderstorms, insects, airplanes, exotic foodstuffs. The list goes on and on, and includes deeply ingrained prejudices which the adult recognizes as unfounded but can do nothing about.

Part of the problem of avoiding the transmitting of our own irrational fears to our offspring is that children are so totally credulous, willing to believe almost anything, especially if it's bad. Parents can do two things. They can try their best to control the expression of their own unfounded fears; some parents can even laugh at their own irrationalities, which doesn't do away with them but at least makes them less infectious for the child. Some children learn to mock their parents' fears. One woman I know is deathly afraid of mice; every time one of her children found a dead mouse, he would wave it in her face. The other thing parents can do is encourage their child in venturesomeness, in a willingness to try himself out, even at the risk of minor hurts, so that he develops a general sense of competence and confidence.

It may help to bear in mind that the child has a number of models to learn from, and that the parents are not the only influences in his life. Children quite early develop a certain amount of objectivity toward their parents, and are remarkably adept at spotting parental inadequacies. It is by no means rare to hear a preschool child either reassuring or ridiculing a parent for harboring an irrational fear. Later on, of course, the child will pick up endless superstitions from his schoolmates; an unsuperstitious upbringing in the preschool years helps immunize the child against some of the more threatening superstitions. (When I was a child, I somehow "learned" that to cut the skin in the fork between thumb and forefinger would bring on lockjaw, and I spent many an anguished hour worrying about it.)

Let us say again that we want children who are neither recklessly brave nor overwhelmed by terrors but who can exercise good judgment. The mixture of prudence and daring probably never turns out exactly right, but we do the best we can.

The Fearful Child

Some children, as we know, are a bundle of fears, all but immobilized by the possibilities for hurt that they sense lurking everywhere. One can easily jump to the conclusion that such children have been overinstructed in the real dangers that the world contains. This conclusion is questionable. What seems more likely is that these children have not been able to grow completely out of infancy because the parents could not convey to them attitudes of basic trust.

On balance, in spite of parental anger, arbitrariness, and blunderings, enough love usually shows through to convince the baby that his parents and the world in general are trustworthy, benevolent, and responsive. In conditions of abuse or neglect, basic trust may fail to appear. When this happens, the child perceives the world as loaded with booby traps, and no amount of reasoning is going to convince him otherwise. People made fearful by their early experience are also likely to carry with them an extra load of resentment and hostility, so what begins as fear may come out as chronic aggression. The only treatment for crippling fearfulness is to reeducate the child in the lovingness and dependability of his parents. If the parents, in their own concrete behavior with the child, cannot provide evidence that the world is basically safe, then they cannot help.

There are those, of course, who say that the only sensible preparation for life in today's world is to bring the child up paranoid. None of us completely escapes paranoia, but pervasive paranoia becomes a self-fulfilling prophecy. Luckily, most of us as children learn enough basic trust to be able to move about and act with some degree of freedom.

TV and the Development of Fears

Much has been made of the violence shown on the television screen and its possible effects on the young child. We hear on the one hand that TV violence will serve as a model for the child, eliciting violent attitudes and behavior. On the other hand, we hear that the child will learn from TV that the world is a violent place in which no security is possible. TV can be a potent influence on the child's thinking and feeling, but it need not be. One can imagine that a child whose life was circumscribed by the world of television would gain a very strange image of reality. But a reasonable amount of regulation by the parents to shield the child from the most noxious programs, plus some shared watching and discussion of the rest, including commercials, soon teaches the child the necessary skepticism. Sensible parents provide alternatives to TV watching, and the tube will not loom large in the lives of children who have a variety of activities and diversions. People blame television for the sins of the larger culture which it amplifies and caricatures so well.

3. THE BABY AS A SOCIAL BEING

The evidence is beyond dispute that babies develop normally only in communication with warm, loving adult human beings. (Don't believe the stories you hear about babies reared by wild animals.) There is no period of a baby's life when he is a mere vegetable, needing only to have his physical needs attended to. From the moment of birth the baby can see, hear, smell, taste, feel pain, and react to changes of position. Immediately after birth, he can make sensory discriminations, and he seems to have built-in preferences for the human face and voice as things to look at and listen to, and for the kind of snuggling and rocking that adults provide as a source of soothing. Although most American adults find it hard to believe, snug swaddling has been shown time and again to have a soothing effect on babies. Babies growing up swaddled have periods outside their wrappings when they can move their limbs, and there is no delay in motor development. Recent research by Evelyn Thoman and Anneliese Korner shows that crying newborns are effectively quieted by being held in an upright position.

Even though the newborn baby may spend as little as four hours a day fully awake (and much of that either squalling to be fed or being fed), during those few hours he is absorbing information about the world and learning what things look, sound, taste, and feel like. From the age of a few weeks, the baby can discriminate faces and voices, and he responds to the sight of his bottle by opening his mouth and straining toward the nipple. But according to the kind of care and attention he gets, he is also learning that people, and through them the world as a whole, are either gratifying, trustworthy, and stable, or else hurtful and unpredictable. Erik Erikson has defined infancy as the period in which the child learns general attitudes of trust or mistrust, depending on how reliably his parents gratify his needs for food, love, and attention. The well-loved, well-cared-for baby develops powerful bonds to his parents, and these bonds are essential to the later communication, including that involved in discipline, that makes further development possible.

Such attachments are not a peculiarly human phenomenon. Newly hatched fowl, such as ducklings and goslings, become powerfully and semipermanently attached ("imprinted" is the word used by biologists) to the first moving object to which they are exposed, whether that object be the mother bird, a football on a conveyor belt, or ethologist Konrad Lorenz. This attachment seems an important ingredient in defining the animal's identity as a member of a particular species, since human-reared fowl select human beings, and not species-mates, as love objects. Harry Harlow's renowned experiments with baby monkeys reared with terry cloth-covered dummy mothers demonstrate how powerful the young creature's love, based on "contact comfort," for even an inanimate "mother" can be. Harlow's studies also demonstrate that love is not enough: monkey and human babies need other kinds of stimulation to develop normally. This emotional learning, which happens within minutes or hours in nonhuman species, takes several months for the human baby. The powerful attachments to a familiar figure who looks and feels and smells just so are, of course, the foundations of stranger anxiety and separation anxiety, which can also be observed in nonhuman creatures.

Parents have many roles to play. Most obviously, they have to take care of the baby's physical needs—to feed him, protect him from extremes of hot and cold, change his diapers, keep him clean, protect him from injury, and all the rest. In the early months the baby's needs for sheer physical care can seem so overwhelming that parents find it hard to bear in mind their other roles. But in fact, feeding, changing, bathing, and the rest can involve the parent as affection-giver and playmate. Talking and singing are two of the easiest and most beneficial things one can do while attending to a small baby. An extra squeeze or caress or pat or kiss is a loving accent to almost any form of caretaking. What one says or sings seems to be of little significance. Variation in tone of voice, however, indubitably helps. Shut away from the rest of the world, you can say and sing things to a baby that would cause you total mortification to say or sing in public. I myself can recall declaiming fragments from Shakespeare, reciting nursery rhymes, talking sheer gibberish, holding forth on the election returns, and singing (more accurately, croaking), "Columbia, the Gem of the Ocean," "Lonesome Road," "Old Man River," and advertising jingles. I also found that I had some limited gifts as a composer of original lyrics based largely on rhymes with my children's names. Many parents, I am afraid, find it very hard to talk to a baby who cannot yet answer back, but I am convinced that parental garrulity from earliest infancy makes an important contribution to forming emotional attachments and to the baby's own later speaking.

According to research by Burton White and his associates, parental competence does not consist of perpetual communication between parent and child. The mothers who were rated as most competent—and whose babies in turn showed the highest level of competence—were those who knew, by whatever intuition, when the baby needed attention, and what kind of attention he needed. In addition, they knew how to flavor every act of caretaking with an extra measure of affection and stimulation.

As the baby matures, other parental roles emerge.

The parent at times must play the role of disciplinarian, teacher, and plaything. But he or she can do all these things lovingly, too, keeping a stable core of identity for the baby.

Social Games of Infancy

Parenthood is a serious business, but this does not mean that it has to be grim. Rousseau is said to have commented, "If you would fulfill your design of forming serious men, you must begin by forming playful children." I have found, much to my surprise, that many people do not understand the idea of playfulness. College students asked to interpret Rousseau's dictum are likely to understand it to mean that children should play a lot. They have trouble grasping that it means an exploratory attitude to life, an awareness of many possibilities in situations, that can be expressed in serious enterprises as well as in frivolous ones.

Thus with parenthood. It is essential in dealing with babies and small children that you be able to unbend, to be aware of the child as a source of pleasure for you, and of yourself as a source of pleasure for the child. Many of the forms of shared enjoyment between parents and babies are spontaneous inventions, while others have become formalized and ritualized down through the centuries. Both kinds are of value, and I make no attempt to categorize in the account that follows.

Before the baby is a couple of months old, there is little one can do in the form of social play except talk to him, snuggle him, and pet him. There is one thing you can watch for, though: when you have his attention, try sticking out your tongue; many babies, from about the age of a couple of weeks, sometimes at only one week, respond by sticking out their tongues. After age two months, you will notice a new kind of response when you talk to the baby, as when you are cleaning or dressing him. He watches your mouth intently, and when you stop talking, he writhes and wriggles and works his mouth laboriously, as though trying to answer back. Once in a while, he even manages to emit some sort of vocalization. You can judge by the baby's muscle tone when he is ready to be jiggled overhead, or swung by the armpits (your hands should clasp his chest, not his upper arms) between your knees. Likewise for wrestling—gently, please!—around on a bed. Even young babies enjoy being drawn into a sitting position by their hands ("Upsy-daisy" is the ritual cry) between the legs of a seated adult. Later, when the baby can sit up without support, he is likely to take pleasure in being pushed over from his sitting position on a soft surface.

It is probably never too early to begin playing "This little piggy," or in general working the baby's hands and feet, although the baby may not come to know his hands as his own until age two months, and his feet until six months. From about four months, the baby can sit up comfortably when propped, and he may enjoy having his face covered briefly with a handkerchief or diaper, in a rudimentary form of peekaboo. By age five months, when he usually can remain sitting up after the adult has put him in place, he will begin to be able to control the cloth, covering and uncovering his own face, and then peekaboo will be truly a delight. Remember that all the ages given here are approximate, and the baby's own behavior has to be your guide.

Age six months is a turning point for social games. By about this time, the baby has gained a great many competences. He is on an eating schedule of three meals a day plus snacks and bottles; he can feed himself some foodstuffs, cramming cereal into his mouth with the palm of his hand or clutching a cracker or apple slice and biting off mouthfuls; he can roll over and sit up by himself; he can probably crawl on his now-plump belly and perhaps push himself up onto hands and knees. Imitation flowers in late infancy. The baby joins in family laughter, even though he has no idea what the joke is, and may try to start his parents laughing again by uttering a strangled would-be laugh. Sometimes parents are baffled by a peculiar gesture the baby makes, only to recall that it is his version of some out-of-the-ordinary activity engaged in by the adult earlier in the day. One example I remember is a girl imitating the motions involved in breaking eggs into a bowl. The baby imitates mopping up spilled liquids with a rag or tissue; he imitates the adult imitating the baby's babbles; he imitates blowing on hot food and blowing out a match; he even tries to imitate the adult's whistle. He learns to puff out his cheeks so that the adult can pop out the air. He learns to use a forefinger to plug and unplug the adult's whistle. Late in infancy he learns a sort of pat-a-cake, though he cannot yet produce a clapping sound, and he waves bye-bye, at first by fisting and unfisting his fingers.

In his high chair or feeding table the baby learns to drop toys, dishes, and spoons overboard, listening or watching for the impact. (I advise a feeding table, since if the baby slides out of his seat, which he is likely to do if the adult forgets to strap him in, he doesn't have so far to fall, and because the extended top of a feeding table gives a baby considerable scope for play.) At first, this dropping game seems to be an exploration in spatial relations, but the baby soon gets the idea that it's fun getting the adult to retrieve dropped objects. It is in picking up things that the baby has dropped that the adult may get his first awareness of the baby's liking for endlessly repeated activities. He may also get an insight into the baby's intrinsic delight in manipulating other people, in getting a rise out of them, in testing different patterns of responding associated with his own behavior (what Frances Horowitz calls "contingent feedback"), and in deliberate teasing. There are obvious limits to adult endurance (one ends the dropping game by moving the baby from the table to the floor—you can try other devices, but I am willing to bet that they will not work), but it helps if one understands the psychological importance of such games. They help the baby define himself as a capable being and the world as partly under his control —the ultimate subtleties of controlling and being controlled have to be worked out over a lifetime, but the process begins early.

Once the baby can creep, new possibilities appear. He enjoys fleeing a parent who cries, "I'm gonna getcha, getcha, getcha," and then scoops him up and swings him. As with peekaboo, the suspense cannot be maintained too long. The creeping baby can hide from his parents, behind a door or a piece of furniture, cackling with anticipation as a parent goes through an elaborate charade, spoken as well as acted, of looking for the baby in all sorts of unlikely places such as wastebaskets and ashtrays. Even without hiding, the baby feigns not to hear himself being called, and sits gigglingly immobile while the parent looks for him everywhere except where he is, perhaps even tripping over him while doing so. Toddlers and preschool children enjoy having a parent go through the motions of sitting on the child, complaining about the lumpiness of the seat and wondering what can be wrong.

In late infancy the parent can begin some teaching of skills. The baby can learn on his own how to switch a radio or TV set on and off, and to regulate the volume, but he can be taught how to work a pull-chain light switch by putting the chain in his hand and moving his hand properly. What the baby may have trouble with is relaxing his pull to allow the switch to reset itself. You can teach a baby through imitation how to use a stick to get something beyond his reach, but you have to do it from behind the baby, so that you draw the plaything to him.

The Parent as Plaything

The relaxed parent, who can get down on the floor with the baby or otherwise make himself accessible, will find that the baby does not always treat him as a fellow-human. The baby will sit on him, climb on him, bounce on him, and treat him as a curious object to be poked, probed, pinched, petted, and explored. By age ten months, babies who have had a lot of experience with mirrors recognize themselves in the glass—an ability found also in chimpanzees. But it is toward the end of the first year or early in the second that the baby really discovers his own facial features, and he does so out of his explorations of the adult's. When he is being changed, for instance, the baby may finger the adult's eyebrows, eyes, lashes, nose, nostrils, lips, teeth, tongue, and ears—the baby turns the adult's head from side to side to see both ears. Especially when the baby wants to feel your eyes, you will have to remind him, "Gently," an admonition he understands and responds to. After a certain number of such explorations, the baby touches first the adult feature and then feels around for his own corresponding one. He has to feel around because these features are not at first precisely localized for him. Again, he is careful to check out both of those features that come in pairs, like eyes and ears. If the adult consistently labels the features, the baby soon becomes able to comply with such requests as "Show me your teeth."

It is interesting that in one sense the one-year-old knows that he has two eyes, but in another he doesn't. Try this test with a one-year-old. Take a cardboard tube, such as the core from a roll of paper towels, and look through it at the baby; hold the tube a little bit away from your eye so that the eye will be illuminated and thus visible to the baby. If necessary, you can call to the baby to get this attention. All the babies I have tried this with find it a delightful game and want to try it themselves. Let the baby have the tube and watch what he does. He will plant the tube squarely between his eyes, as though he experiences seeing as centered in a single cyclopean orb. Babies younger than a year seem unable even to try, and some one-year-olds end up with the tube at nose level. It is around age two that babies place the tube over just one eye.

A word should be said about lap-sitting in toddlerhood. The toddler does not try to climb into the adult lap, but offers himself to be drawn up. Once there, he may snuggle briefly, but his usual style of lap-sitting is a highly active one. Lightly encircled by the adult's arms, he rocks and sways, leans backward as far as possible, and eventually straightens his body and slides to the floor.

Preverbal Communication

Long before he can talk, the baby finds ways to let his parents know that he wants something and what it is that he wants. Initially, of course, he simply cries, not with any intention of communication but as an automatic expression of something's being wrong. As we shall see when we discuss sleep, by age two months the baby uses a controlled kind of crying to protest bedtime. By about nine months, the baby shrieks as a way of telling people that he wants something, leaving it to them to guess what it is. If the desired object is within sight, the baby may strain toward it. At a later age he points. When he can move around, the baby uses concrete enactments to convey his wants. He tries to climb into his feeding table as a sign that he wants to eat; still later, he may hand the adult a phonograph record that he wants to hear played, or he brings his coat as a sign that he wants to go out. Notice the similarity here to the dog who brings his leash to be taken for a walk or his food dish as a way of asking to be fed.

Less obviously, though, parents have to learn to respond to a host of behavioral cues akin to the dog's wagging tail. They learn to read the baby's "language of behavior," which tells a parent what a baby needs or wants. Thus, the parent learns to distinguish the quality of cries, to read gestures and postures, and to get a general notion of what the baby is expressing. A certain amount of trial and error is inevitably involved, and the feedback the parent gets from the baby—a grunt of relaxed contentment, a sharp turning away—signals whether the parent is on the right track.

As we shall see, well before the baby has begun to speak, he becomes able to understand some part of what is said to him. He can follow such simple instructions as "Please hand me my socks." He scoots toward the bathroom at the announcement "Bath time," and he claps his hands in response to "pat-a-cake." What is more, some infants give evidence of seeking words. They point to something and make an interrogatory sound, such as "Duh?" Supplied with the thing's name, they give a small satisfied grunt. All in all, two-way communication begins early in those cases where parents can take the time to pay attention and learn to be sensitive to the baby's unarticulated meanings.

Relationships with Other People

The parents, at least in our society, are usually the first people with whom the baby has social relations, but the roster of people he knows expands rapidly during the first few years. Obviously, different families provide greater or lesser scope for knowing people outside the home, but almost all babies have some acquaintance with relatives, family friends, neighbors, baby-sitters, and doctors and nurses. Babies do not always cotton to new people right away, and the wise person takes his time in getting to know the baby. Nowadays, on a small scale, there are babies born into communal settings who have multiple caretakers, and perhaps some built-in "siblings" right from the start. I am not prepared to make any statement on how communal sharing affects the child; from some comments I have heard from communards, though, one should choose your fellow commune-dwellers with at least the care given to selecting a mate. There are many gradations between full communal sharing and families living isolated from each other, and almost any arrangement, short of bringing up a "closet child," seems to offer opportunities for sound development. While you will want to shield your baby from people with acute infections, it hardly makes sense to shut the baby off from contact with other people. He will pick up occasional sicknesses, but these are inevitable, and all children have to go through a period of building up immunities.

One problem that some parents manufacture, even as they try to prevent it, is extended overdependence on the adult. What most parents do not realize is that the baby weans himself emotionally when he is ready to. The way he becomes ready is by being given abundant love and support in infancy. Parents who try to force a small child to be self-reliant are actually producing insecurity and a need to cling even harder. This, of course, is the stuff of which vicious circles are made. The important thing is to instill basic trust during infancy: the trusting infant turns into a toddler striving, if ambivalently, to be autonomous. By age two and a half or three, he will have become a preschool child who is indeed capable of a certain amount of independence. Just to keep things in perspective, though, you should bear in mind that we never totally outgrow our dependency, our need to look to others for emotional support.

Peer Relations

Most parents want their children to develop friendships, to share and cooperate, to learn to love, and to take satisfaction in human relationships. As in the case of independence, this is a process that cannot be rushed. It takes several years for a child to recognize other children as fully human, and it does no good to moralize about the child's lack of fellow feeling. It will come, but its coming will have very little to do with parental measures other than their letting it happen. Two infants set down near each other are likely not even to notice one another. If their eyes meet, there most certainly is no shock of recognition. One baby may try to explore and manipulate the other, but only as an exercise in idle curiosity.

Toddlers from about fifteen months to two and a half years carry the acquaintance process a step further. They seem dimly to recognize a shared identity. They stare at each other, reach out tentatively to touch, and circle each other. The stage of preliminary inspection may end with a hug, by one toddler's handing the other a plaything, or by one toddler taking the other by the hand and leading him to show him something. All this in silence. Toddlers rarely speak to each other except in anger, when they may shout "No!" or "Mine!" They do, however, enjoy each other's company, and play contentedly side by side. Property disputes do arise and are usually settled by a grim tug-of-war, the loser bursting into tears and seeking adult solace. It does no good to scold children of this age for their selfishness or to exhort them to share. Rather, one works out a routine of taking turns; when it comes time to transfer possession, the children have usually forgotten the dispute.

Children of preschool age, about two-and-a-half onward, are capable of complex peer relations. They fight, they brag, they share their ideas about things, they make up games and fantasies, they cooperate with each other. The shift in peer relations is often signaled to the parents by the child's producing some tidbit of information that they know did not come from them. From age three on, one can recognize some basic (but by no means unchangeable) social orientations: the resolutely independent lone wolf, the sidelines onlooker, the leader, the manipulator, the clinger to adults, the child with a chip on his shoulder, the gregarious child who nevertheless bites when frustrated.

There are some well-defined patterns in the way play with peers develops. Two-year-olds play side by side, taking pleasure in each other's company but interacting minimally; this is called "parallel play." Around age two and a half, the children, still with very little interaction, begin doing the same thing at the same time: painting, playing in the sandbox, "telephoning," climbing on the jungle gym; this is known as "associative play." From age three on, we see "cooperative play," which involves a great deal of communicating and sharing of ideas. Among the many things that three-year-olds like to do together is having a conversation. Try eavesdropping on such a conversation, and you may be treated to what Piaget calls a "dual monologue": the children speak in turn, each listening politely until the other has finished, but what one child says bears absolutely no relationship to what the other is talking about. Although they observe the form of a conversation, each child is delivering his own private soliloquy. Another favored activity among preschool children is dramatic play, the acting out of scenes and episodes based on everyday life.

Obviously, no child is ever going to be fully worthy of your child's companionship, but for the most part we have to go along with the child's own choice of friends. Once in a while, though, the child forms an attachment to a friend whom the parents find unspeakably obnoxious. It is probably just as well to avoid communicating your feelings to your child, but it is a simple enough matter to think of reasons why you can't have so-and-so over to play today. Or any other day, for that matter. The friendships and enmities of the preschool years are highly unstable, and children can always find a new object for their fickle affections.

No matter how sophisticated the preschool child seems to be in dealing with his peers, he still has his emotional base in the family. He still wants to be cuddled, the bedtime rituals must still be observed, he wants to hear stories (sometimes the same ones again and again), and he wants to talk with his parents about such recurring themes as God, Santa Claus, fairies, dreams, and where babies come from. He may still suck his thumb or a pacifier at bedtime, and he may be unable to sleep without his favorite doll or blanket to curl up with.

Preschool?

Parents of preschool-age children repeatedly ask whether their child should attend a preschool or play group. The answer is simple: It depends. A well-run preschool can give a child a lot of satisfaction. The beneficial effects for the child are greatest when he has limited opportunities for emotional and intellectual learning at home, when there are few playmates available close by, and when his attachment to his parents is so powerful that it is very hard to leave him with sitters. A good nursery school can help ease clinging to parents, provide playmates with whom to try out ideas and ability to cope with conflicts, and stimulate a great deal of learning of all kinds. But—the child is not doomed to lifelong social and academic failure if he cannot go to a preschool. The benefits to be gained from attending preschool can, with a little effort, be provided for at home.

The real reason for asking about preschool, though, is often somewhat different. It is this: Am I betraying my trust as a parent and risking damage to my child if I ship him off to a preschool so that I can have some time to myself, to work, to get the housework done without incessant interruptions, to loaf and watch the telly, to entertain my lover? The answer is no, provided you can find a good school. It takes the expert about fifteen seconds to smell out a really dreadful preschool, and perhaps half an hour to realize that a school that superficially looks good is really not worth much. The ordinary parent should allow several hours in the classroom to get the feel of a school, although it is a rare school that will permit so long a visit.

When looking at a preschool classroom, watch first for whether the atmosphere is cheerful—bored, aimless children are as much a warning signal as squabbling ones. In a group for two-and-a-half-year-olds, the number of children per teacher should not be much above five. With older children, one teacher can manage with as many as eight or ten. Observe the extent of teacher involvement; the teacher who simply monitors the group or who organizes activities from on high is to be avoided. Stay away from schools which lack abundant playthings and equipment, or which stringently ration playthings and materials and activities for fear of "overstimulating" the children. Observe how involved the children are with each other; you can always expect to find a couple of children playing alone, but anything approaching universal isolation is ominous. Check the sanitary arrangements and safety features. But above all, try the atmosphere on for good vibrations. A good preschool atmosphere reflects both relaxation and a high level of focused activity. And while observing, remain unobtrusive, so that you do not become an alien and disruptive presence.

A final word to parents who have a child in preschool. Try to avoid the common blunder of asking, "What did you do in school today?" This question makes no sense to the child, who was busy living his life, not keeping a record of events. All you can do is wait patiently, knowing that if there were salient episodes, pleasant or disturbing, they will come back to the child, if only in the context of bedtime stalling.

Sibling Relations

There is one other form of social relations that may be important for your child. This is the matter of how he is likely to feel if a new baby arrives. Folklore has long recognized what Alfred Adler formalized as the notion of sibling rivalry, which points to the "dethronement" of a first—and hence, for a while, only—child by a new baby brother or sister. Jealousy is the rule. It may be expressed in a variety of ways, from an outright assault on the intruder to suggestions that he be flushed down the toilet or returned to the hospital, to surreptitious punchings and pinchings when the parents are not looking, to regression, or a return to more infantile ways as though to compete with the baby on the baby's terms.

Jealousy probably cannot be prevented—even the family dog may show resentment of a new baby—but it can be minimized. Some parents make the mistake of not telling the child that a new baby is on the way. The sensible course is to tell the child enough in advance to let him get used to the idea and raise whatever questions he may have, but not so far in advance that the whole business becomes unreal with the slow passage of time. Remember that time passes much more slowly for children than for adults. The child can be given a share in the preparations for the new baby, with the idea of conveying that it is the family's baby and not just the parents'. He should be prepared for the mother's stay in the hospital and the perhaps unprecedented separation. A familiar adult should be ready to stand in for the father while he is hanging around the hospital waiting for the birth.

However much attention the new baby commands, it should not be to the exclusion of the older child. Friends who bring baby gifts might bring something for the older child. The older child should be encouraged to handle the new baby, to pet it, and to share in its care (you will have learned by this time that newborns are not easily broken). A child of three can help bathe and dry a baby, he can give it a bottle, and he can rock it to sleep. If the care of very young babies is painful drudgery for adults, it can be a fascinating form of dramatic play for a preschool child.

It is important, though, to make sure the older child has some attention that is exclusively his. If need be, let mother or father take him completely out of the house, to go on an outing, to eat dinner at the hamburger stand, to visit friends or relatives. Try to keep the older child's routines intact. If he has a bedtime story, make sure he gets it. The new baby will keep the parents worn out for a while, but they still have to do right by their first-born.

One special issue is raised by giving the new baby the breast. The mother can, if she wishes, breast-feed away from the older child, but most of the young women I have talked to prefer to return to the openness and naturalness of breast-feeding a generation or two back. The older child will be fascinated, will ask endless questions that have to be answered as frankly as possible, and there is a good chance that he himself will want to nurse. Only if the mother can do it totally without embarrassment or awkwardness should she agree to nursing him. Obviously, there is nothing wicked about putting a three-year-old to his mother's breast, but the idea would make many people uncomfortable. If this is the case, one simply tells the child that nursing is for tiny babies, not for a big boy or girl like you.

If, in spite of all your efforts to give the older child his due and to minimize jealousy, he nevertheless tries to assault the new baby, he can be restrained firmly and even angrily without any implication that he is bad or depraved. Ordinarily, "Gently" sets the tone both for the parents' dealings with the children and for the older child's dealings with the new sibling, but if necessary one can be rigidly categorical: "You must not hit the baby!"

4. SLEEP, FEEDING, ELIMINATION, AND SCHEDULES

The mechanics of child care should not be allowed to become mechanical. Caretaking routines offer some of the very best opportunities to establish good emotional relations between parent and child. It is in the course of giving the baby a bottle, or bathing him, or changing his diapers, that one has the chance to talk to him, cuddle him, sing him songs, and all the rest.

The first general question is that of regularity, of getting the baby on a schedule. This issue used to loom large in manuals of baby and child care and still is a prominent theme in advertising for laxatives. Foreigners view our preoccupation with time, schedules, and punctuality as something of a national mania. Fortunately, the behavior of young people indicates that the mania may be dying down. What many parents fail to realize is that stabilization of body rhythms is the norm, that instead of trying to force the baby onto a schedule, one nudges him toward the family pattern in cooperation with normal physiological trends.

All animals and many plants develop so-called biological clocks, so that there is a daily cycle of wakefulness and repose, hunger and satiety, digestion and elimination; even one's body temperature follows a daily schedule. You can become aware of your own biological clock by traveling east or west a considerable distance by jet; you then feel how your own functioning is out of phase with your new surroundings. The biological clock gets set by the rhythms of the environment, but it becomes semiautonomous and follows its own rhythms until reset by changed circumstances.

Stabilization of body functions is thus desirable—for the mother so that taking care of the baby will take its place among other pursuits, and for the baby so that he will have times of physiological quiescence during which he can become involved with the people and objects around him. But a schedule is not something to be rushed, and there are different timetables for stabilizing sleeping, eating, and elimination. And stabilization of body functions is not the same as being in thrall to the clock.

Sleeping

It comes as a surprise to most new parents that newborn babies sleep as much as twenty hours a day. It seems less because the baby wakes so often and noisily. One may have to watch closely to be aware that there are brief periods, between eating and sleeping, when the baby is alert and receptive to experience. Otherwise it might seem that the baby is either asleep or howling with distress, or, mercifully, just nursing.

At first, the baby's sleep patterns are closely linked to his hunger patterns, and he gets hungry around the clock, demolishing his *parents'* accustomed sleep patterns. Even when the newborn baby is asleep, his parents cannot be at rest: as we have seen, inexperienced parents are likely to hover over the bassinet, expecting every noisy breath to be the last.

Most babies, beginning at birth, show a distinct preference for lying on either the back or the belly, and they let you know when you have placed them in the less favored position. Back-sleepers are likely to develop a bald, flattened area where skull meets mattress. The flattening and baldness go away—although some flatness may persist—when, after about age six months, the baby begins varying his sleeping position.

77

As you probably know, dreaming is marked by changes in the brain waves and by rapid movements of the eyes. Newborn babies show the physiological signs of dreaming —you can watch the rapid eye movements, or REM, happen behind the baby's lids. In fact, newborns show a greater proportion of REM sleep than people of any other age. What, if anything, newborn babies dream about I cannot say.

In the first few months after birth, the baby begins to stay awake for longer periods, although it may take much of the first year for a stable pattern of well-defined morning and afternoon naps to emerge. Three other important changes take place in sleep patterns during infancy.

The First Bedtime Crisis

The first big change in sleep patterns is a new reaction to evening bedtime, beginning at about two months. At earlier ages, when put to bed, the baby whimpered and fussed briefly and fell asleep. Now, he seems to recognize evening bedtime as the end of play and companionship —he will still get fed during the night, but his parents are unlikely to feel particularly playful or sociable—and he resists, crying at full volume. There is a new feature in his crying, though. It has become an instrument of communication. If the parent, thinking that something serious may be wrong, stops moving away from the baby's sleeping place, the crying stops momentarily. If the parent remains stationary or, reassured, resumes moving away from the baby, the baby starts again to cry, at first in short bursts but increasingly in long, loud howls.

There are several ways of managing this crisis of bedtime. What one does *not* do is repeatedly go in to the baby, checking him to make sure that he has not vomited, that he has no fever, or that a diaper pin has not been left open. Whatever one does, it has to be done decisively.

There will come a time, sooner or later, when the baby has to be allowed to cry himself to sleep. It takes fifteen or twenty minutes the first night—and subjectively, those fifteen or twenty minutes can seem to stretch out into a lifetime. However, it will take somewhat less time on successive nights, until after three or four nights the baby will go to sleep without crying. The guilt-ridden parents will be surprised to find that they have neither traumatized the baby nor sundered the bonds of affection. The following morning, the baby will be just as delighted as ever to greet his parents.

This exercise of total parental authority has to come. Indeed, it may have to be repeated after almost every period of illness when parents are obliged to go in to the waking baby during the night. But the moment of truth does not have to come right away if the parents do not feel that they are up to it (they will rationalize their feelings by saying that the baby is not yet up to it, but no matter).

There are two interim devices you can use. One is to let the baby fall asleep in the middle of the family's continuing activity, moving his bassinet or carriage to his regular sleeping place after he gets to sleep. There are two disadvantages to this technique. First, moving the baby may reawaken him and start the process all over. Second, once the baby gets used to falling asleep in the midst of bustle, he may later find it very difficult to fall asleep in conditions of quiet. It is for these reasons that I recommend the alternative strategy of having a parent stay with the baby awhile after putting him to bed, perhaps patting the baby's back or crooning softly or gently rocking him until sleep comes. This procedure has the obvious disadvantage that it ties down for as long as half an hour an adult who is undoubtedly fatigued and who has plenty of other things to do. Thus, you pay a price for procrastinating; it is your decision, but you should decide in full awareness that you are only postponing the inevitable. Whatever course you follow, don't forget that a soft light left burning in the baby's room often helps to reassure him that the world is still there.

Sleeping Through the Night

A second change in sleep patterns, beginning at around three months of age and lasting for several weeks, is giving up nighttime feeding and sleeping through, from perhaps eight in the evening to five in the morning. There are two ways of knowing when the baby is ready for this transition. First, he consumes substantial quantities at each daytime feeding and is able to go several hours between meals. Second, when he wakes up for nighttime feedings, he seems less interested in nursing than in having a period of play and sociability with his parents.

Although he gives signs that he is now able to sleep through the night, the parents will have to use some gentle persuasion to get him to do so. First, they should not respond to his cries unless they become truly persistent. If they do have to respond, they should try soothing or rocking the baby back to sleep without giving him a feeding—never mind that his diaper is wet, since *he* doesn't. Finally, if a feeding does seem to be called for, it should be given in as unstimulating a way as possible. If the baby is given a bottle, for instance, he can be propped up slightly in his bassinet or crib and allowed to nurse from an adult-held bottle. The first time he expels the nipple, the session should be considered at an end. Burp him gently and put him back to bed. If he cries, you will know it is not for cause and you can ignore him. After two or three weeks of the cool treatment, he will lose interest in the whole business and sleep undisturbed. The parents' disposition will improve considerably.

The New Style of Waking

During the first few months of the baby's life, parents get accustomed to being awakened in the morning by the baby's screams. He is hungry, he wants company, so let the servants come. Then, one morning when the baby is about four months old, the parents awake with a feeling of disorientation. It takes them a minute to realize that for the first time in months they have waked up of their own accord rather than in response to their human alarm clock. The silence seems almost ominous. As they come to, though, they realize that the silence is not total. From the direction of the baby come sounds of crowing and gurgling. He is lying awake and amusing himself. If the parents peer in quietly at the baby, they will find him squirming around to survey the ceiling and upper walls, picking away at the designs on his crib bumper (babies apparently see two-dimensional patterns as though they were solids), and playing with his hands, vocalizing all the while. When he spots his parents, he smiles at them affectionately but shows no signs of wanting to be picked up right away. Some babies, indeed, resist being picked up until the time of solitary play has run its full course. This change has a dual meaning. In practical terms, it means that the parents will henceforth get a little extra sleep in the morning. In psychological terms, it indicates that the baby has reached a new level of self-awareness and self-sufficiency—autonomy, if you will.

Programing Sleep

Parents, like other people, come in two versions, larks and owls. The early-rising larks will have little trouble coming to terms with their babies' sleeping patterns. The nocturnal types, though, will want to nudge their baby toward a sleep schedule more consonant with their own. This can be accomplished only within limits. One can gradually shift the baby's bedtime to a later hour, and he will slowly come to sleep a little later, but by owl standards the baby is still a confirmed lark. Take heart: by the time he is six or seven years old, he will be able to get his own breakfast, and the parents will have to get up only in time to see him safely off to school. By adolescence, of course, the youngster is likely to become a super-owl who wants no part of bedtimes and has to be dragged bodily from the sheets in the morning. Fortunately, such matters fall outside the compass of this book.

Dreams and Nightmares

Sigmund Freud proposed that the function of dreams is wish fulfillment. In sleep our guard is lowered and all our repressed fantasies come out of the basement. When these become too wild they take the form of nightmares which wake up the sleeper. Thomas French proposed a major revision of Freud's view, relegating wish fulfillment to second place and emphasizing instead the integrative function of dreaming, whereby the previous day's happenings are worked over during sleep and made part of our personal history. Nightmares, of course, would represent events that resist assimilation, either because the events are too dreadful or because to assimilate them would twist our self-image beyond recognition. French's view fits very well with recent research on dreaming and dream deprivation. We have learned that there are physical indicators of dreaming, and volunteers can be waked up selectively—between dreams, right at the end of a dream, or right at the beginning of a dream. Individuals consistently awakened just as they start to dream soon show serious fatigue, disorientation, and irritability, which could be attributed to lack of opportunities to assimilate experience. I have long suspected that the reason parents feel so awful during the first few months after their child's birth is dream deprivation rather than simple loss of sleep.

We have already seen that newborn babies at least go through the motions of dreaming. In later infancy, there are indications that dreams have content: the baby mumbles, groans, and moves around in his sleep. Babies even have occasional nightmares and wake up screaming in terror. If these become the rule, it probably means that the baby is being stimulated beyond his ability to make sense of and integrate his experiences through dreaming, and I would advise that the pace of his activities be slowed, with increased time for cuddling, rest, and quiet activities.

It seems almost universal that the nightmares of preschool children are peopled by witches and giants. One could blame the fairy tales that children are told for supplying these images, but there is reason to believe that fairy tales themselves express some deep psychological impulses. The witch often seems a surrogate for the mother or stepmother, and the giant a symbol for father. If one puts oneself in the place of a scared child being yelled at by angry, powerful adults, it is easy to imagine how his dreams can take shape as witches and giants.

I might mention, incidentally, that when babies and young children get sick, they are prone to raging fevers. These fevers may produce delirium, hallucinations, and other psychological effects, such as highly sharpened perception. How to deal with infections is your physician's business. The matter is noted here to help you understand what otherwise might seem most bizarre behavior.

Where Babies Sleep

Nowadays, many babies born in the hospital are carried home in a disposable bassinet, and a number of perents simply use this as a bed for the first few months. Nothing elaborate is called for, but babies do take comfort from feeling enclosed. In our family we had good luck with a hand-me-down folding carriage, the body of which lifted out to become a baby basket and car bed. By about three months, the baby outgrows his bassinet and is moved to a crib or cradle.

It is ordinarily not much before three years that the child is ready to sleep in a bed. Many youngsters are reluctant to leave the security of their familiar crib in favor of a bed, even though the bed symbolizes a new maturity. The shift can be made gradually and in many cases has to be. The child may not much care for the wide-open feeling of a bed, and it takes a while for him to get the hang of not going over the edge in his sleep. Children rarely injure themselves falling out of bed, but it can be an unsettling experience for child and parent alike. Thus, take it easy. Let the child try out the bed for his naps. Let him alternate between crib and bed. He himself will eventually opt for the bed, especially if you remember to tuck him in snugly. And don't trap yourself in a new bedtime crisis by being in a hurry to sell or give away the crib. If moving from crib to bed coincides with the arrival of a new baby, the change could have either of two meanings for the child. It could signify his new mature status, which sets him off from the helpless, squalling intruder. Or it could represent displacement, having to give up his accustomed ways to make room for the newcomer.

Starting early in infancy, the baby clutches, fondles, and may suck on a corner of his blanket as he settles to sleep. His blanket is likely to be a well-loved token of security. Like Linus, your child may want to carry his blanket about with him, hugging it for comfort in moments of stress. Parents used to be prone to interpret such attachment to a blanket as psychopathological. They may still be repelled esthetically, especially if the child is unwilling to relinquish the blanket to have the stench laundered out of it. The baby can be deprived of his blanket long enough to have it washed and dried, but otherwise

I favor letting him have it as much as he wants while he is at home. He will get over his attachment to it. (It is worth mentioning in passing that Harry Harlow's experiments with terry-cloth mother monkeys were suggested to him by baby monkeys' evident love for the cloths used to carpet their cages.) In addition to his blanket, your child will undoubtedly have one or more dolls or stuffed animals that he hugs at bedtime. The baby can manage very well to hug a doll or two, suck on his blanket, suck a thumb, and twist his forelock or finger an ear as he drops off to sleep.

Many parents keep a first baby in their bedroom for a month or two, on the mistaken assumption that they might otherwise fail to hear the baby if something were to go wrong. Their increasing faith in the baby's power of survival, together with a desire for privacy, then usually dictates moving the baby to his own room. If space is at a premium, the parents may surrender the bedroom to the baby and make the living room their sleeping quarters.

Whenever it is possible, giving your child a room of his own is the least troublesome path. And if a second child comes along, it is nice if he or she can have a private bedroom. In a great many cases, though, such lavish use of space is not possible, and one makes the best of what one has. Two or more children may have to share a bedroom. If the children are twins, they are likely to get caught in a spiral of reciprocal stimulation that makes getting to sleep very hard indeed. Parents of boy–girl twin pairs also seem concerned about later sexual involvements between brother and sister.

If the children are of different ages, it is best to make sure that the younger one is asleep before putting the older one to bed—which incidentally helps emphasize to the older child that he holds a special position in the family. As children grow into the preschool years, they develop pronounced cravings for privacy, and deep possessiveness about their belongings, so it is a good idea to give each child his or her special space. There are a number of ways of marking the boundaries of the reserved spaces, but a solid barrier like a bookcase makes the division clear.

If, like many other parents, you are cramped for space, you will have to face the problem of being caught in the sex act by a toddler or preschool child. Most parents find the prospect embarrassing, and take elaborate precautions. Others are yielding to the preachments of people like Paul Goodman who advocate total openness about sex, even to making a point of letting your children witness you making love. The notion here is that our much-discussed sexual shortcomings are a product of sexually repressive and secretive upbringings, and the antidote is to emulate those non-Western people who sleep together as a family. In theory, the parents wait for the children to fall asleep before having sexual intercourse, but the anthropologists tell us that children regularly witness parental sex. This early exposure seems to do them no harm and may even enhance later sexual experience. On the other hand, watching one's parents copulate is by no means necessary to sound sexual development, so don't feel pressured to do something that goes against your cultural grain. Whatever one may theorize about sexual openness, our early emotional training is likely to rise up and haunt us.

Sleeping Away from Home

There will be more to say about traveling with babies and young children, but here some mention should be made of possible sleeping problems. The style nowadays is to cart the baby about in his bassinet, a baby seat, a sling, or a backpack, and the babies nap quite comfortably in any of these while their parents bicycle about, visit friends, go to the movies, or dine out. However, sleeping overnight away from home, especially in late infancy and toddlerhood, is less simple. The baby will probably have to sleep in a borrowed or rented crib in unfamiliar surroundings. You may well groan, but here once again comes stranger anxiety—and insomnia.

If you are staying with friends, they may have thoughtfully provided a separate room for the baby to sleep in. As tactfully as possible, decline this option and place the baby's crib where the adult action is going to be so that the baby can see and hear his parents. Chances are that he will be far less of a hindrance to the adults than he would be screaming his head off in another room. The crying-himself-to-sleep routine does not work, or works only after some hours, when the cause of his crying is fear rather than simply not wanting to go to bed.

Be sure the child has his security blanket and accustomed bed toys. They serve the baby as talismans of home and stability. Without them, his usual patterns are all the more seriously disrupted. Don't be ashamed that they smell bad. Your baby needs them.

Eating

It is not my purpose here to advise you on problems of nutrition. Your pediatrician will outline a sound diet and you will try out a lot of things for yourself. As long as you can obtain wholesome food in adequate amounts and prepare it appetizingly, your baby will probably flourish. I am concerned rather with some of the psychological issues that are constantly being raised by parents and Experts.

Breast or Bottle

A great deal of emotion still attaches to the question of whether babies should be raised on the breast or the bottle, and fanatics can be heard propounding theories in favor of one or the other.

It seems to me that there are only two main things to be said. If you are poor or live in highly unsanitary conditions, breast-feed your baby, and continue to breast-feed him as long as possible, even though he also eats solid foods as well. That way, you will be providing him with the best diet possible. If you are reasonably well-off and live in reasonably sanitary surroundings, the only possible advice I can give you is to do what you want to do, and to do it without embarrassment or self-consciousness or guilt. Some women find great sensuous pleasure and emotional satisfaction in nursing their babies. Others find that they can get much the same satisfaction from giving a bottle. Some women produce milk in great abundance, others have a marginal milk supply, and still others an insufficient or erratic flow. In any event, it doesn't make you any more of an animal than you already are if you decide to nurse, and you are not raising a plastic child in a plastic world if you choose bottles.

It seems fair to summarize the pros and cons of breast-feeding. I have already spoken of the psychological pleasures some women find in nursing. Human milk seems to be one of the highest-quality baby foods around. It appears that mother's milk contains antibodies against disease, since breast-fed babies don't get sick as much as bottle-fed ones. With breast-feeding, one avoids all the mess of bottles and formulas and sterilizing, although much of this mess is obviated if you can afford to buy prepackaged formula in disposable bottles. Finally, nursing mothers are less likely to get pregnant than non-nursing mothers—lactation is not a foolproof contraceptive, however, so please do not blame me if you play Russian roulette and lose.

On the negative side of the matter, nursing mothers complain of chronic fatigue. They tend to gain weight, and American women are reluctant to think of themselves as other than svelte. One reason that lactating women may escape getting pregnant is that some males find them less than dazzling sex objects. Even at the risk of sexual alienation, men might well promote breast-feeding, because it is the one chore that men cannot share in. In other words, the woman who breast-feeds is stuck with the entire job of feeding the baby, night and day, seven days a week, for several months. One can slip in an occasional bottle, or even a run of bottles—if the baby will accept it. Once he has learned the characteristics of the breast, he is likely to reject substitutes. All in all, then, you have to make your own choice, with both husband's and wife's feelings the main consideration. The question of weaning the baby from the breast will be taken up under the general heading of weaning.

You will be told before leaving the hospital that you should feed your baby on a schedule, every three hours if yours is a small baby or every four hours if he is large. Unless you are the lucky parents of a very exceptional baby, you will rapidly discover that this is impossible. Some young babies seem to have had their fill after taking only a couple of ounces of formula. What is more, they tend to vomit up a sizable proportion of what they consume, either in the course of being burped or spontaneously (vomiting as a part of motion sickness doesn't appear before late infancy). You soon find yourself trapped in a sequence of small feedings at very frequent intervals. It is essential to break out of this routine, but to do it in a way that takes account of the baby's still-unstable digestive tract.

The trick is *gradually* to space out the feedings, to give the baby a chance to get really hungry so that he will eat more and thus be able to wait longer for the next feeding. You cannot, of course, just let the baby scream for an extra half hour or so while you are delaying his feeding, but there are ways to distract him from lesser hunger pangs. Gently rocking him in his carriage is one, rocking him in your arms and talking to him is another, and holding a pacifier in his mouth is yet another, although not all babies will accept a pacifier. Sooner or later, the distractions will lose out to the clamor from the baby's gut, and nothing will stop his crying except to feed him. It is quite amazing to see how abruptly the redness drains from his skin and his sobs subside once he has a functioning nipple in his mouth. In a month or so, you can induce the baby to eat on some approximation of a three- or four-hour schedule. By age six months, most American babies are on a regular three-meals-a-day (plus bottles and snacks) schedule.

Most psychiatrists and psychologists, including me, feel that it is extremely important to hold the baby while giving him his bottle. Feeding is an unparalleled opportunity for parent and child to get to know one another. The baby typically stares at the adult's face while nursing, and adults are usually moved to stare back, to talk and croon to the baby, and to get as much pleasure from cradling a small body as the baby gets from being cradled. Once the baby has begun smiling to faces and voices, at around age six weeks, he likes to stop sucking occasionally and beam up at the person holding him. Later on, toward age one year, the baby enjoys holding his own bottle and may resent the confinement of being fed by an adult.

Feeding gives you an opportunity to observe a couple of cognitive changes in the baby. At first, the way to get the baby to take the nipple and begin the complex built-in sequence of sucking, swallowing, and breathing is to touch the nipple lightly to the region of his mouth. Without this concrete contact, the baby seems unaware of the bottle. By contrast, by the time he is a month old he opens his mouth when he sees the bottle. Learning to recognize the bottle on sight is an achievement, but less of one than it appears. Holding the baby in the feeding position, try showing him something other than the bottle. The chances are that the one-month-old will open his mouth in response to just about anything. Over the next few months he becomes more discriminating and will open his mouth only to a nursing bottle with the nipple properly aimed.

A second cognitive change comes at about four months. This is shown in the baby's ability to wait to be fed: once the adult has picked him up, the baby stops crying and holds himself tensely. You can feel the tension of self-control in his muscles, and some of it overflows in bleats and whimpers and straining with his body toward the place where he is fed.

Sucking

It is important to realize that sucking is more than just a way to get sustenance. Babies have a need to suck for the sake of sucking. Freudians interpret the baby's need to suck as evidence for oral eroticism, but it seems simpler to think of the mouth as an important sense organ through which the baby gets a great deal of information about the world. Many adults have oral needs not too different from the baby's. Smoking, gum-chewing, gnawing on erasers or wads of paper, and perhaps overeating, all serve to allay oral cravings which may be a carryover from an infancy in which our sucking and chewing urges went unsatisfied. If the baby doesn't get enough sucking in the course of nursing, he sucks on other things, most notably his own thumb. (Putting new objects into his mouth is probably not related to unsatisfied sucking needs, since all normal babies do it.)

One way to help babies get their full quota of sucking is to nurse them with slow-flowing nipples, so that they have to do some extra sucking to get a normal amount of milk. One can, if one so desires, spend a good many hours piercing nipples with a hot needle to get just the right flow, but most people are put off by the smell of burning rubber and the difficulty of knowing when one has made the hole the precise size needed. It seems to make better sense to feed the baby with ordinary nipples, and if he seems to need a lot of additional sucking, to buy a few pacifiers. Up to age four or five months, the baby will be unable to retrieve his pacifier when it falls out of his mouth, and you have to have a set of spares in reserve.

The baby's urge to suck becomes further complicated by an urge to chew on things when teething begins, from about age six months until about two and a half years. The pacifier may suit the baby's needs, but some babies prefer something more solid to chew on, such as a smoothly sanded clothespin (the one-piece wooden model). The need to suck and chew is most pronounced at bedtime, when the baby withdraws into a self-contained state in anticipation of sleep.

It is no good worrying about the baby's sucking of the thumb or pacifier. The various cures that have been offered don't work very well, and they ignore the psychological need for sucking. If the baby is given all the sucking opportunities he needs, he will give up daytime thumb and pacifier sucking—except in moments of stress—by about age two, and by two and a half he can be talked out of taking his pacifier to bed. Sucking is a need, not a virtue, and as a need it shouldn't last forever. He may not outgrow his favorite bed toy or security blanket until the school years, but that is another matter.

Weaning

It used to be the case that weaning was thought of as an occasion of great turmoil and perhaps even trauma. A more modern view of the baby tells us that weaning, if carried out gradually and in a relaxed manner, need cause no trouble at all. "Weaning," of course, refers to several different things: weaning from the breast, weaning from an exclusively liquid diet to a predominantly solid one, weaning from bottle to cup, and weaning from baby food to a regular diet.

Let us begin with weaning from the breast. I had not thought of this as any particular problem until I talked to several young women who were in considerable conflict about when and how to stop nursing. One of the babies involved was crowding age two. There seems to be a myth abroad to the effect that the truly devoted mother nurses indefinitely, and that weaning the baby from the breast too early—a time nobody could define—would do him untold psychological injury.

Except for mothers living in poverty or in seriously unsanitary conditions, breast-feeding will ordinarily have served its psychological and nutritional functions by the time the baby is six months old. The nursing mother should bear in mind that the baby begins to get teeth at this age, and once he has teeth he bites, not out of malice but because that is what his teeth tell him to do. One can even observe babies chewing on their milk before swallowing it. By this age, the baby should be eating quite a few foodstuffs besides mother's milk, and nutrition should be no problem.

The baby may at first be reluctant to take a bottle, particularly if he has not been given any practice with this form of nursing, but relaxed patience on the part of parents will bring him around. It is conceivable that the six- or seven-month-old could be weaned directly to taking the milk from a cup, especially the kind fitted with a spout, but babies at this age find it hard to manage milk in doses larger than what they get by sucking on a nipple. Besides, a cup does not provide the sucking the baby still needs.

Solid Foods

Now let us backtrack a little and consider the introduction of solids into the baby's diet. Obviously, we are not really talking about solids that have to be bitten and chewed, but about the varieties of mush that babies get fed, whether it is bought in jars from a manufacturer (check the label for additives), puréed in a blender, or prechewed and spat into the baby's mouth.

Most pediatricians nowadays recommend that solids be tried out from an early age—three or four months—not so much because the baby needs them as to get him used to taking food in this novel form. It is a good idea not to begin a feeding with solids; a hungry baby will have no truck with experiments. Let him nurse awhile to take the edge off his hunger. Then try slipping in a little mush—cereal, fruit, liver, whatever—on the tip of a spoon. The baby will react in one of two ways. He may cry lustily and spit out the food as quickly and thoroughly as he can. This is a signal to the parent to stop for now. You can try again at the next feeding, perhaps with a different food. Fruit, alone or mixed in with other foods, is likely to tickle his taste buds. There is no way to know whether the baby is reacting to solids in general or just to this particular flavor, but babies do have strong taste preferences. The second kind of reaction involves grimacing, rolling the food around in the mouth, and losing quite a bit of it in the process, and maybe even swallowing some of it. If this happens, let him have some more. If he refuses a second taste, clamping shut his mouth and averting his head, wait a minute and try again. If you can take a few seconds for introspection, you will find that you are working your mouth as though to induce the baby to do likewise. Keep feeding him as long as he will accept it, but when he clearly has had enough, stop until next time. Forcing, or attempted forcing, will only raise the baby's resistance and complicate the whole business.

Once the baby has gotten used to eating solids, and you have learned about his preferences, you can begin trying new foods. Babies like to try tidbits from the adults' plates, and once they are able to pick things up, they enjoy gnawing on a cracker or apple slice which they can hold themselves. Even earlier, they may like to grab a fistful of mush and cram it into the mouth with the palm of the hand. Babies take pleasure in exploring the physical properties of foodstuff. They like to pour and dabble and smear, using food for fingerpaint. I counsel permissiveness and patience. This is one more component of the baby's learning about the world he lives in and his capacities for control and manipulation. When the baby has finished playing with his food, he will want his hands and fingers wiped clean. This is not an expression of some primordial guilt; rather, his sense of touch is impaired by residual goop.

The baby will not be able to feed himself with a spoon until he is well over a year old, but long before that he wants to try. His efforts along this line will reduce the efficiency of the feeding process, but efficiency is less important than good communication and the development of competence. He will try to grab the spoon as it approaches his mouth. A relaxed parent will find that he can share management of the spoon with the baby and still get him fed, regardless of spilling.

At a slightly later age, the baby can be given his own spoon to hold. In the beginning, he will use it mainly to dip in and out of the dish, occasionally raising it to his mouth to suck or lick off whatever food may be clinging to it. Over the months, he will become more expert and can take over more of the job. Bear in mind that when he is eating true solids, like peas or bits of meat, he will ordinarily use his fingers. At age eight or nine months he develops a pincers grasp with thumb opposed to forefinger, and will take great joy in picking up tidbits and popping them into his mouth.

Feeding Problems

It is becoming rarer, but one still hears about children who "just won't eat." This description is obviously inaccurate, since children with "feeding problems" survive and grow, which starving children do not, but it cannot be denied that a certain number of children eat very little or restrict their diet to a very few foodstuffs. One child I knew lived exclusively on milk and chocolate-covered graham crackers for several years and, surprisingly, stayed healthy.

There are probably some physical disabilities to account for some feeding problems, but the overwhelming majority seem to exemplify the working of the self-fulfilling prophecy. It is precisely those mothers—and it usually seems to be the mothers—who are afraid of feeding problems, or who are grimly determined to avoid them, who have children with feeding problems. For such mothers, mealtimes are charged with anxiety; the anxiety shows up in the way they feed the child, and the child responds by losing his appetite. The more the mother urges, cajoles, or tries to force the child into eating, the more disagreeable the idea of eating becomes to him. Feeding problems in themselves do not seem to be important: it is as expressions of a disturbed mother–child relationship that they become troubling.

Pica (The Eating of Non-foods)

It is a commonplace that babies are "all mouth" and that anything they encounter is likely to end up in the mouth. In addition, a great many babies actually eat things that do not qualify as food. Some of these things are harmless. Some, in fact, are culturally approved and esteemed, as in the case of clay, which is a regular part of the diet of some Americans, particularly in the South. Others, though, are definitely harmful and even lethal, and the baby must be protected against them. Kitchen compounds, medicines, paint and the associated fluids, insecticides, and all the rest have to be kept out of the reach of babies and young children. In too many slum environments, of course, not even perpetual vigilance can keep the baby away from lead-bearing chips and flakes of putty and paint, and an undetermined number of poor children have, and will continue for untold years to have, some degree of lead poisoning.

Just to be on the safe side, you should keep by your phone the number and address of your nearest poison-control center.

The fact of pica leads us to consider more closely the widely known but poorly understood phenomenon of the *wisdom of the body,* first enunciated by the great physiologist Walter Cannon. Body wisdom says that we can recognize at some appetitive level the presence in foodstuffs of nutrients in which our bodies are deficient. Rats kept on salt-free diets, for instance, drink a weak saline solution in preference to plain water. A famous study by Clara Davis on self-selection of diet, "Cafeteria-feeding," by newly weaned babies is often cited as evidence for body wisdom at the human level.

There seems to be little doubt that children given an array of nourishing food to choose from can select for themselves a reasonably balanced diet. Unfortunately, there are three ways in which the wisdom of the body is an imperfect guide to eating. First of all, as stated above, it does not warn us away from poisons. Second, our normal appetites get blunted by excessive intake of sweets. Third, whatever our organic proclivities toward a sound diet, it is our culture that defines food and non-food for us, with very little regard for good nutrition. Thus, body wisdom is vital to non-humans, but it is of limited utility to people living in traditional cultures or in an environment loaded with synthetic chemicals.

Toilet Training

Most parents can take pleasure in feeding a baby. What happens at the other end of the digestive tract is all too likely to be a source of considerable unpleasantness. Here again we are likely to be the prisoners of old cultural attitudes, which view elimination as disgusting, and perhaps even vaguely sinful, fit only to be brought under control so that it can be kept hidden away. There is also an implicit folklore that says that the baby uses elimination to manipulate and humiliate his parents. In fact, sensible parents who can suppress their aversion to urine and feces, and who can adapt to the baby's biology, find that toilet training goes rather smoothly.

Yesteryear's attitudes emphasized the necessity for toilet training at an early age. Today's attitude are more relaxed. Almost everybody seems to know that you have to work with the baby's maturation to do the job effectively. Some people, though, have taken the Freudian view to mean that toilet training is injurious to the child, while others have bought a Romantic-Naturalist notion that sphincter control happens spontaneously if only you wait long enough, and these people simply do not train their children or wait until it is too late. The results in some cases are most unfortunate.

There seems to be a *critical period* for toilet training, during which it happens easily but before and after which it becomes increasingly difficult. The exact ages vary from child to child, but eighteen to twenty-four months can be taken as a rough norm. In any case, one does not go by the calendar but by the behavior that tells you when the child is ready.

We have to begin by recognizing that toilet training involves three somewhat different processes with somewhat different timing: bowel control, waking control of the bladder, and sleeping control of the bladder. Timing is of the essence. For one thing, all use of the pot in the early years is done seated, and training cannot even begin until the baby is old enough to sit up comfortably. More than this, though, the baby cannot learn control until he becomes aware of his own elimination.

Arnold Gesell proposed, and experience supports him, that awareness comes in three stages, not counting the earliest stage of seemingly total unawareness. First, in late infancy, the baby becomes aware that he *has* eliminated. Later, he becomes aware that he *is* eliminating. Finally, he becomes aware that he *is about to* eliminate. It is only at this last stage of awareness that training is likely to accomplish anything enduring, so the best we can hope for during infancy is some preliminaries that get the baby used to the pot and the idea of eliminating therein.

It helps, too, if the baby is free to observe his parents using the toilet. Once the baby can creep, he will trail everywhere after his parents, and he enjoys watching their bathroom functions. The odors of elimination bother him not a bit. The one problem with this learning through observation and emulation is that both little boys and little girls may want to urinate standing up, like Daddy, and may have to find out the hard way that it will not work.

Bowel Control

Many babies develop a regular schedule of defecation in late infancy. As often as not, this elimination on schedule happens while the baby is asleep, which helps not at all. When, however, the baby has a regular schedule of waking bowel movements, he can be put on the pot when the movement is due. If he resists, don't fight it. If the bowel movement does not appear as scheduled, don't keep the baby confined to the pot. If he does defecate into the pot, express your pleasure with moderation. If the procedure works, and he is willing to cooperate, some helpful preliminary learning has been achieved. Notice, though, that it is the parent who is trained, not the baby. If the baby's digestive rhythms shift, it is the parents who have to adapt.

Even when the baby's bowel movements come at irregular intervals during his waking hours, the parent can often see and smell them coming and put the baby on the pot. Remember that the idea is not rapid training but rather to get the baby used to the whole business. And it should be a pleasant getting used to. The parent can keep the baby company while he is on the pot, or give him something interesting to play with, or, at later ages, provide him with a picture book to look at. If the baby leaves the pot without eliminating, expressions of distress or sorrow or anger are decidedly out of order.

A couple of practical considerations. If possible, get the baby a sturdy potty chair rather than a baby seat that fits on a regular toilet. There are two reasons why a potty chair is to be preferred. First, the baby will be able to get in and out of it himself, an important consideration in any cooperative venture. Second, many babies are frightened by the elevation of a toilet seat or by the noise of flushing waters. Most babies form an attachment to their familiar toilet setting and find it hard to eliminate without the customary apparatus. This means that when you go traveling you have to take along the potty chair, which makes it much less convenient than a miniature seat, but one learns to face down the supercilious bellboys.

A number of parents have asked me for my opinion about disposable diapers as compared with cloth ones. I cannot imagine what psychological difference it can make. Disposable diapers do add one more complication to problems of solid-waste disposal, though, and, in terms of cost, diaper service should be about as cheap.

Casual early introduction to the pot is helpful in setting patterns, but some children simply will not cooperate. One sometimes has to wait until the child can be told and can comprehend that he is too big to go in his diapers. He will need a lot of reminding, but if parents persevere, the baby will learn.

Waking Bladder Control

The signal that the child is ready to learn waking bladder control is that he begins to stay dry for ever-longer periods. Beginning at this point, the child should wear training pants instead of diapers when he is awake. Diapers will continue to be a sleeping necessity for a while. The parents become able to intuit when the child has stayed dry long enough and is ready to wet, and they can then invite him to use the pot. Boys are likely to have an erection just before urinating, so first the parent, and later the child, must aim the penis downward, lest he spray the landscape. If the boy resists sitting on the pot to urinate, there are alternatives. One can remove the pot from the chair and hold it for the boy to urinate into. On auto trips, a paper cup makes an effective urinal for a little boy. Either boy or girl can be set astride the family toilet, facing the tank, which gives the child something to hold on to and brace himself with. Even though the girl has fewer interesting possibilities than the boy, girls learn, and without visible signs of penis envy. Daytime bladder control usually is well established by age two and a half, although most children hate to interrupt their play to go to the toilet, and accidents are by no means rare as late as age four.

Sleeping Bladder Control

Once the child has gained reasonably full control over his urinary sphincters while awake, sleeping control seems to follow pretty much automatically. Some parents like to wake up the baby to urinate before they themselves go to bed. This may help, and it does no apparent harm. Obviously, though, it is a practice that cannot go on in-definitely, and parents should know when to stop, perhaps when the baby begins protesting.

Notice that we have been talking about a period of almost two years in the baby's life. Toilet training goes hand in hand with the child's physical maturation, and there is no point in trying to rush it. I do not know if the anal character traits described by the Freudians are in-deed related to overly severe or overly lax toilet-training techniques. I think it more likely that they reflect a whole complex of early experiences. But there is available a middle path to the control over elimination which is com-patible with all the other attitudes of love and trust and autonomy that parents wish to impart, and it seems sense-less to let toilet training become the occasion for great emotional upheavals. Parents have to bear in mind, too, that slips will continue to occur for several years at times of special excitement, stress, sickness, or in response to who knows what factors. Lapses should be taken in stride, but children can still be reminded that they are too big now to wet the bed as a regular thing. I would recom-mend, though, that you keep a rubber pad on the bed for several years.

When Bladder Training Fails

I have never heard of a normal individual who failed to learn to control his bowels. There are quite a few adults, however, who still do not have urination under firm control. We can sometimes guess about the psychological causes of failure to learn bladder control, but in many cases the reason eludes us. When a child in the school years still wets the bed without any other obvious physical or psychological dislocations, conditioning techniques may be called for. I have had no direct experience with such techniques, and have heard of both good and unsatisfac-tory results, so the decision to try them is up to the parents. The principle is quite simple. An electric circuit is set up in the bed so that urine wll close the circuit and set off an alarm that awakens the sleeper. The idea is that the bladder tension preceding urination becomes a conditioned signal to wake up and go to the bathroom.

5. DISCIPLINE

The subject of discipline is one that churns up tremendous ambivalences in modern parents. Public figures declaim against the evils of "permissiveness," and parents have an image of nihilistic children destroying the house, family belongings, and other children; practicing sadism against small animals; and eventually, joining a band of urban guerrillas. Parents hear educators warn against stifling the child's creativity, of the crippling dangers of harsh discipline, of turning the child into the robotlike slaves to convention which most adults are. The child may drive parents to furies of frustration, such that they wonder about the merits of exposing children on the hillside—and then reduce them to a mass of sentimental jelly, so they think the child can do no wrong and the worst possible fate would be to lose this small creature's teeming affections.

It seems to me that the problems and conflicts parents have with respect to discipline and control reflect a basic uncertainty about what the parents really believe in. It is not my business to dictate parental values, although my biases will be obvious, but parents may find it helpful to try to think through their own feelings. One device, first suggested by Mary Essex, that works very well with college students, is to supply endings for a series of incomplete sentences. Both parents might try completing the sentences independently and then compare the results. The sentences are:

1. I like children who———.
2. I dislike children who———.
3. When I was a child, I liked grownups who———.
4. The most important thing for a child to learn———.
5. I wish my parents had———.

Your sentence completions may strike you as unremarkable, and even self-evident, until you compare them with somebody else's, like your spouse's. Consider especially the way you completed sentence 4. The themes that have emerged most prominently from the responses of college students are such things as obedience and respect for authority; learning to get along well, to fit in, and to be well liked; independence, in the sense of not being a burden to others; and way down the list, autonomy, in the sense of being able to think and decide for oneself, self-fulfillment, and creativity. Note what is missing. It is a rare event for anyone to mention explicitly religious themes, such as putting one's faith in God.

No one, in my experience, has mentioned the themes of competitive striving, acquisitiveness, and materialism which many observers contend dominate life in American society. It is clear, though, that conformity to social norms ranks high, and differentness ranks low.

There is, however, another way, if you prize autonomy, creativity, and, eventually, intellectual competence. You have to begin by ridding yourself of metaphysical notions of morality whereby the Right Way was either divinely decreed or has evolved through social trial and error. A modern view of morality is based less on tradition and more on what makes sense in terms of good human relations. This view stresses compassion, cooperation, understanding, and respect for individuality. Such an outlook is communicated primarily through the way parents deal with their child, and, later, through the example parents set—in today's terminology, the models they provide —in their dealing with other people and things. This approach is in no way incompatible with the exercise of parental authority. The important thing is for parents to understand why it is necessary to exercise authority.

The Phantom Issue of Permissiveness

Not only do most public figures denounce permissive child rearing and education, they blame it all on the influence of Dr. Benjamin Spock. Their denunciations reveal two things. First, they have not read Spock very carefully. Spock is a very moral man with a solid belief in authority. He is wise enough to know, however, that excessive authority alienates those on whom it is practiced and in the end becomes self-defeating.

The second point revealed by such denunciations is a view of human nature as anarchically self-centered, so that it must be defused and thwarted before it escapes and looses chaos upon the land. This view overlooks the helplessness of human infants, their reliance on the good will and good offices of their caretakers, and, above all, the human need for love, approval, and attention. One can make babies into monsters of ruthless egotism, but it isn't easy.

Assuming that isn't your goal, you should give the child scope for exploration, experience, discovery, and mastery, meanwhile protecting him against danger, protecting the parents and their most cherished possessions against the child's clumsy inquisitiveness, curbing the child's sometimes unruly passions, and trying to impart the foundations of a humane morality. Out of such morality comes self-control, the ability to modulate one's own search for satisfactions in terms of other people's needs, and ultimately to seek out shared satisfactions.

Discipline and Basic Trust

Erik Erikson has pointed to infancy as the period of life in which the child comes to view the world as a place that is safe, nurturing, reliable, manageable, and rewarding or, contrariwise, full of threat, treachery, unpredictability, and forces beyond control. These two outlooks have been summed up by Erikson in the terms "basic trust," corresponding approximately to optimism, and "basic mistrust," or pessimism. These attitudes, learned in infancy from lessons forever lost to memory, can color one's perception of persons, situations, and events throughout life.

Most parents, in the course of meeting the baby's basic physical and psychological needs, instill, without thinking about it, attitudes of basic trust. The bond that is formed is essential to the exercise of meaningful parental authority. Without basic trust, the baby, engulfed by his own misery and insecurity, is insensitive to parental feelings.

The trustful baby is alert and responsive to variations in parental feeling, including feelings of disapproval. Indeed, even when parents try not to disapprove, as when reason says to leave the baby alone but the viscera say no, the baby will respond to the subtlest kinds of cues—tensing of the parental muscles, a quick intake of breath, a strain in the voice, whatever. For instance, all babies get themselves into situations of mild danger, where good sense says that they should be given a chance to work things out for themselves but parental anxiety dictates immediate intervention. On another plane entirely, the baby's explorations of his genitals are an important part of coming to terms with his body, but many parents cannot resist an upsurge of moral dread. The baby, at some primitive level of perception, detects these reactions and incorporates them into his understanding. Thus, parents

109

can never do an ideal job, and have to resign themselves to communicating at least a residue of inappropriate feelings. These are not vital in a general context of basic trust.

Basic trust comes in several varieties, though, and it is important to understand the components. Most fundamental, of course, is the baby's trust in his parents and through them of the world at large. Never mind that he will meet betrayal, and that his basic trust will come to be tinged with skepticism, doubt, and, eventually, a measure of cynicism. He has to begin with a virtually limitless belief in the solidity and reliability of his parents. In addition, though, parents have to learn basic trust in the baby. They have to trust him to solve some of his own problems, to endure some setbacks, and to become, gradually, self-reliant. But for this to happen, parents have to trust themselves, their concern for the baby, their responsiveness to his needs, their own sense of what is right and wrong, and their ability to function sensibly. Finally, of course, the baby has to learn to trust himself, to feel good about himself, to feel competent, open, curious, and capable of giving love as well as receiving it. All this takes time, of course, but it begins in infancy and depends on the sensible regulation of the baby by the parents. We cannot escape the need for regulation, so we should approach it thoughtfully.

Discipline and Punishment

One difficulty in talking about discipline is that many parents unthinkingly equate it with punishment. They shrink from the idea of punishment, but they cannot conceive of alternatives. There *are* alternatives. There is the use of concrete and social reinforcers, as advocated by B.F. Skinner. There is encouragement as well as admonition. There is setting a good example for the child. And there is, as his verbal skills and understanding expand, explanation of why some course of action is preferable to another. But let us first face up to the bugaboo of punishment.

Let me begin by saying that punishment has its limited uses, and when punishment seems the method of choice, one should use it without hesitating. But this statement is meaningless unless one understands something about punishment. Punishment embraces a variety of things. For instance, punishment is not necessarily physical. There are many forms of psychological punishment, from verbal deterrents and warnings and threats to deprivations, scoldings, shaming, and humiliation, and on to the withdrawal of love and attention. Psychological punishment, it should be obvious, can be as devastating as physical punishment. In fact, most adults would take quite a bit of severe physical pain in preference to a very small amount of verbal castigation. Physical punishment can range from a mild slap on the hand or bottom to lethal brutality. Obviously, punishment—physical or psychological—should never be more severe than warranted, and the parent who feels his rage outrunning his self-control *should stop short*.

Punishment should be based on three really important principles. First, it should be used only when there is no other way to communicate a prohibition to a child, which means that punishment can be used only to restrain the child from doing bad things and never to teach him to do good ones. Second, you must be able to control the timing. Once a misdeed is done, punishment is a waste of time and emotion. If you cannot catch the child *in flagrante delicto* or, better yet, at the very beginning of a forbidden act, punishment will have only undesirable effects. The child has to be able to connect the punishment with his action, as a direct and immediate consequence, or its meaning is lost. Even if later punishment inhibits the act, it is liable also to be less specific and to inhibit other, perhaps unrelated acts. Mistimed punishment simply teaches the child timidity, resentment, and evasiveness, so that he may wait until he thinks he can get away with the misbehavior. One further principle applies. Too much punishment simply inures the child to the whole idea, and so loses its effectiveness. To work at all, it has to stand out as a rare event.

Although punishment, or "aversive control" as the behaviorists would have it, has some limited utility, other means are preferable. Reward, or positive reinforcement, helps shape and maintain desirable forms of behavior. Note, though, that most of the things that you want your child to do are intrinsically rewarding, and only in special cases, where the child has had to put in some extra effort, are additional social rewards like praise and applause called for. When what the child does is merely annoying rather than wrong or dangerous, non-reinforcement— ignoring it—may be the answer. Certainly, to display one's irritation serves as a reward by giving the behavior undue attention, which provokes the child to further provocation and perhaps makes a showdown necessary. Showdowns are sometimes inevitable, but they should be avoided where possible. In most cases, the adult has to win the showdown, or else the child is encouraged to keep probing the limits of adult tolerance. Losing a showdown, however, can bring great humiliation to the child, and it is heartbreaking to see a baby lose face.

The middle course between escalating provocation and a showdown is distraction, finding something else for the child to do that is satisfying for him and at least neutral for the adult. One ever-available form of distraction, of course, is to play a game with the child. Finally, as we shall say often, there are the techniques of control that set the child an example and help him understand how people get along with each other.

Keeping the Child from Physical Injury

Once the baby is able to move around under his own power, he is exposed to more dangers than the uninitiated parent can easily imagine. For his own sake, the dangers have to be reduced to a minimum, and he has to be taught to avoid those that are a fixed part of the household. Among the largely indispensable features of a modern house are electrical outlets, stoves, radiators, lamp cords (the baby doesn't see that a tug on the cord may bring the lamp crashing down), cleaning compounds, medicines, tobacco, alcohol, and matches and lighters. Some of these can be kept out of the child's reach, but his reach expands rapidly as he becomes more mobile. For instance, one little girl solved the problem of how to reach the top of a bureau by pulling out the drawers in such a way as to form a series of steps. Most babies of toddler age (eighteen to thirty months) can figure out how to move a stool or box to stand on and reach an elevated surface. Various safety latches are available, and one can cover outlets with specifically made plastic caps, but these are as much a nuisance to the adults as a deterrent to the baby.

The best way to proceed is to set definite taboos on certain objects and locations, such as the medicine cabinet and the place in the kitchen where the cleaning compounds are stored. The way to communicate a taboo is with a sharp bark of "No!" the instant the baby begins to reach toward a forbidden object. Timing is vital. If the baby is already in contact with the object, your *no* will be much less effective. If he is already actively involved, your prohibition is not likely to have a lasting effect. This means a period of heightened vigilance until the basic taboos have been established. The parent has to be conscious at all times where the baby is and what sorts of mischief he is likely to be getting into. Once the baby has learned the taboos, parents can be more relaxed, even though babies have an almost infinite capacity for finding new possibilities for trouble.

You should be aware that the baby is not going to accept taboos passively. A number of repetitions will be needed, and you may have to back up your *no* with a sharp slap on the wrist to let him know that you mean business. Even after the taboo is clear, he will still test the limits occasionally, either seriously, to see what he can get away with, or playfully, to tease—teasing seems to be a deeply ingrained tendency among all the higher animals. In these cases you have to reassert the taboo and be prepared to divert the baby to something else.

Let me emphasize that too many taboos are confusing and hard on the baby. You have to childproof the baby's environment as much as adult convenience can tolerate, and beyond that, you have to put up with a certain amount of mess. It is only a few things that have to be strictly forbidden for the child's safety. Otherwise the dwelling should be his playground, for him to investigate and experiment with and learn about. The ordinary household contains what Fred Strodtbeck calls a "hidden curriculum"; it is through his explorations of his everyday environment that the child builds basic conceptions of objects, substances, space, and cause and effect. Too many restrictions deprive the child of the benefits of the hidden curriculum.

A whole new set of menaces lies in wait outdoors. Lakes, streams, and oceans are attractive and deadly to young children. Babies, in their innocent probings and pokings, easily provoke dogs to bite and cats to scratch. The baby does not see cars and trucks as machines to mangle him, and wanders carefree into the street. Parents should make sure that the baby riding in a car always wears a harness, preferably the kind that allows him to stand, sit, or lie down even as it anchors him to the seat. This is because babies and young children do not adapt to changes of speed or direction, and a sudden stop can smash the baby against the windshield, or a quick turn send him hurtling across the car. Even older children, if they are as careless about seat belts as their parents, have to be reminded to stay seated and to hold on.

Another menace of the great outdoors is its built-in invitation to wander afield, and a considerable number of babies and young children get lost. Most of them eventually are found again, but not without great distress to both parents and themselves. The outdoors also contains many things, from litter to weeds, that the child may be tempted to sample—one little boy I know had to have his stomach pumped out on the suspicion that he had been eating the mushrooms that grew in his yard. What all this adds up to is that children cannot be safely left untended out of doors unless they have a securely fenced area cleared of hazards. A secure fence is one that is sturdy, with childproof gate latches, and it is also one that the child cannot climb. I know parents who do let their wee ones out into an unfenced yard without harm, but my heart shrivels whenever I see such children drifting into the street or hear the local teen-agers careening by in cars and on motorbikes. By eliminating the worst dangers, you do away with the need for many taboos, which could make the child excessively fearful.

Protecting the Environment Against the Child

We have been talking about protecting the child against threats from his surroundings; here we must acknowledge that he himself is capable of a certain amount of destruction. Most of the damage a small child does is accidental —he is too weak or clumsy to cope adequately with whatever he is investigating—but this is small solace to parents who see prized possessions lying in ruins. Children can also do harm to their parents' peace of mind and to the physical and psychic welfare of pets. Here again, regulation is called for, bearing in mind that the child needs freedom for exploration, and that apple-pie neatness in a house is incompatible with having a small child on the premises.

As with dangerous things, the basic principle is to move those valuables which are not in frequent use out of the child's reach. The knowing visitor will detect the "high-water mark" that separates the child's play space from the forbidden zone. Vulnerable possessions, like dangerous ones, can be taboo, but there is a difference. Children can and should be given a controlled opportunity to handle the fragile things they find attractive. This is done by seating the child on a cushioned surface and placing the object in his lap. He will perceive from the adult's manner that careful handling is called for, and this can be reinforced with the admonition "Gently"; this may seem a difficult concept for a child to grasp, but in fact he gets the sense quite readily. He can also understand, as needed, "Not in the mouth." The parent will have to stand by, both to help the child in his manipulations and to intervene when the child tires of the object and decides to try flinging it into space.

The case with pets is more complicated. Dogs and cats, as I have said, can be very jealous, after the manner of an older sibling, of a new baby. Usually their interest overcomes their jealousy and leads to affection. In the rare cases where this does not happen, the baby may have to be protected against the animal—it may even become necessary, although it is a painful step, to get rid of a pet. In the more usual case, the family animal shows a remarkable tolerance for the baby's clumsy gestures of curiosity and affection. This is quite different from the strange dog or cat wandering by, which may have very little patience with the ways of babies. Nevertheless, the pet may sometimes need protection, too. In general, the "Gently, gently" approach works best, conveying to the baby that the animal is vulnerable. Pets occasionally do some disciplining on their own, and a growl or a hiss may

very effectively communicate to the baby that he is t̶
gressing.

Let me repeat, because it is important, that restraint̶
on the baby have to operate in a context of considerable
freedom to explore, to try things out, and even to suffer
some bumps and bruises and minor fights as the price of
learning his way around. Parents may even have to restrain themselves from coming to the rescue. A father tells
how his less-than-two-year-old son once slipped from the
edge of a swimming pool into the water. The father's first
impulse was to plunge in and fish him out, but he forced
himself to wait and see. The baby sank clear to the bottom, but then came bobbing back up and took a grip on
the rim of the gutter. He cried briefly and then was very
pleased with himself for having managed on his own.
Children need a chance to try out themselves and the
world, and parents have to put up with some of the strains
and heartaches and headaches it entails. Well-loved children are not willfully destructive, and even at their clum-
siest can do little real damage to the furniture and the
pots and pans and utensils. Give them old paper to crum-
ple and tear and scribble on. Let them dabble in water
and mud and slop around their food a bit. It makes extra
work, but nobody promised you that parenthood would
be easy.

Dawdling

One frequent source of exasperation that parents can
do very little about is the child's dawdling. Doing anything with the baby or young child takes an eternity,
since the youngster seems unable to stay focused on a
goal and to move systematically to get there. But that is
exactly how it is—even though the baby's bodily rhythms
have stabilized, clocks and calendars and schedules and
the synchronization of activity are completely beyond
his ken. He gradually comes to terms with time, but the

117

most basic intellectual grasp takes years (even some adults may not understand our conventions for partitioning time), and to be serious about turning away from the attractions of the moment to follow a schedule or keep an appointment comes very hard indeed to the small child. Adults simply have to allow an extra ration of time to cope with the child's distractibility. While the adult is collecting his belongings or slipping into his coat, the child may be removing his outdoor clothes; it is never until the child has been zipped into his snowsuit and hood that he tells you he has to use the toilet.

The parent may tolerate the child's incurable dawdling better if he can realize that to the child, grownups are the ones who are the incurable dawdlers. If parents can take time to listen to themselves, they will appreciate that much of the child's life is lived to a refrain of "Not now," "Soon," "Later," or "In a little while." These adult stallings and delays are probably well justified, but to the child they seem just like dawdling.

Tantrums, Temper, and Aggression

One aspect of personality that has to be brought under firm parental control early is temper and associated aggression. Some children become chronic hitters, pinchers, kickers, and biters. One thing to watch out for here is your own unadmitted amusement or admiration. You may, without realizing it, be reinforcing the child's displays of temper by very subtle signs of liking his "spirit." Another thing to beware of is fear of the child—I have seen parents literally cringe and cower before a raging child, which may also provide a kind of reinforcement. The best treatment for tantrums is to ignore them. No matter how violently the child flails and throws himself about, he is most unlikely to injure himself.

Here is a mother's account from *Three Babies* of tantrums at age sixteen months:

Ruth has tried tantrums to get her way. She lies on the floor and cries. If I ignore her and leave the room she stops crying, comes to the room I am in, lies on the floor and screams. I go into another room and she follows. When she discovers she cannot get any attention this way, she comes over to me, puts her head in my lap and puts her arms around my legs and says "Hug."

The last way to respond to a tantrum is with a tantrum of your own. I have seen parent and child in a screaming match that escalates to almost inevitable violence, followed by temporary exhaustion. I predict without hesitation in such cases that the pattern will be repeated many times.

Angry children may bite or strike out or scratch or kick. The best way to deal with physical assault, on you or somebody else, is to use firm but soothing restraint. Envelop him in an embrace that keeps him from continuing his attack. This will tie him down but also be reassuring. If a child becomes chronically assaultive—which should not happen if you are reasonably vigilant and keep assaults from occurring—you may, as a very last resort, have to use punishment. If you come to this extreme, it should be made clear to the child that it is the outrageousness of his behavior that drives you to measures of which you basically disapprove. Bear in mind the rules of effective punishment. The punishment must be painful but harmless. It must be so consistent as to seem a built-in consequence of this form of misbehavior. Especially important, the punishment must come right at the beginning, just as the child is gathering himself to pounce. If the child has already struck the blow or sunk his teeth into his victim, the punishment will do no good. By all means, though, try not to allow the child to reach this point; for his sake and yours, you want his upbringing to be as thoroughly loving as you can manage. You will inevitably get angry, as will the child, but if you can control your anger, he will learn to control his.

Morality and Moralism

As parents, we want to cultivate our children's moral sense, but we don't want either ourselves or our offspring to be moralistic, prone to indignation and outrage over every trifle. The foundation of morality is not tradition— what the Wise Men tell us or what Everybody knows— but love and caring. This does not mean universal loving. After all, there are plenty of people in the world who are not the least bit lovable. It does mean, though, erring on the side of charity and compassion in our human judgments, a readiness to give people the benefit of the doubt, and an awareness that the least lovable people probably got that way because they weren't loved enough or in the right way.

Teaching humane morality begins in the way we care for our own child—the way we feel and communicate, in deed and gesture and tone of voice, our respect for the child and his sense of worth. As parents, we inevitably get angry and may even swat and slap our children, but if our basic relation is love and respect, these interludes are harmless. The important thing is that we can show anger or disappointment without feeling or expressing contempt. One can regulate a child through sanctions, violence, and fear, but in so doing we produce a fearful, hostile, violence-prone person.

Much as I disagree with B.F. Skinner on some fundamental issues, I concur most heartily with his view that effective regulation is based on positive reinforcement. There are occasional emergencies that call for the child's immediate and unquestioning obedience, but in general, the adult can stay in charge while making allowances for the child's dawdling, his imperfect or even distorted understanding of situations, and his need to feel in control of his own destiny. When the child can talk, it makes good sense to listen to his side when there is a difference of opinion. It sometimes turns out that the child is right and the adult wrong, and the parent should be able to concede error without having his ego demolished. Reasoning with very young children is seldom of much help, but when the child demands reasons we should be prepared to give them. Sometimes our reasons are less than noble —we want the child to obey because we are tired or out of sorts or preoccupied with something else—and we have to be prepared to admit as much.

Morality deals with things that count, like the child's dealings with a younger sibling or the family pet. There are many areas of behavior that will become matters of moral concern later on but which lie outside the moral sphere for babies and young children. The child's curiosity about his own and other people's anatomy may be embarrassing but it is not wicked. Many parents nowadays have come to take it for granted that the baby may observe them nude or even feel the interesting regions of their anatomy. This openness seems to satisfy the child's curiosity without breeding precocious prurience. Parents have come to take it for granted that babies and young children masturbate, and become concerned only when it seems to be an overwhelming preoccupation.

Children have always inspected each other's genitals, but parents no longer think it a mark of depravity. Similarly, we have come to appreciate that young children's fantasies are very different from telling lies, and that children's ventures into lying are generally caused by fear rather than by any desire to gain an advantage over others. It takes children quite a while to learn manners and courtesy, and meanwhile we have to put up with a directness that can be disconcerting but which we sometimes hate to suppress. My daughter once asked me to explain that "funny-looking" person, the first nun she had ever seen, but I was more embarrassed than the good sister. Much more awkward was the time she asked loudly about a rather masculine-looking woman of my acquaintance, "Daddy, why is that man wearing a dress?" Children are show-offs from an early age, especially those who get a lot of attention and applause for their accomplishments. Here again no moral principle is at stake, but tendencies to show off can be curbed if parents restrain their enthusiasm for the more conspicuous exhibitions.

Modeling

If we accept love and caring as the foundations of morality, it follows that our most effective teaching is not going to be through aversive conditioning or the precepts we preach, but in the example we set. One of the most potent forms of learning is that which takes place through modeling, adopting the actions and styles and feeling tones of the important adults and older children in one's life. Thus, if a parent truly wants his child to be caring and compassionate, he will have to set an example with his own behavior.

One of the most reliable relationships that can be drawn in child psychology is that the child who screams a lot has a parent who is a chronic screamer. All parents shout from time to time, but the parent whose automatic reaction to crises, major and minor, is to yell will most assuredly have children who shout.

I am opposed to all but the most sparing use of physical punishment because of the example it sets. I must concede, however, that there are times when a quick, angry swat on the bottom is very effective and does less damage to the child's sense of worth than other, subtler means of control, such as the withdrawal of love. It is brutally devastating to tell a child, "If you do that, I won't love you." Even the most secure child will not be able to detect the falsity of such an assertion (it is unimaginable that a parent could stop loving a child because of any but the most depraved forms of misbehavior). Parents need to retain authority and be prepared to back it up, but if they have succeeded in forming a close, loving relation with their child, the occasions for invoking authority are blessedly rare.

Besides serving as a model for the child, parents can learn to listen carefully when the child wants to give voice to his moral dilemmas. When the child begins to open his heart, this is the signal to put moralism aside and try, above all, to listen and understand. The patient listener may not have to provide answers. With the parent as sympathetic sounding board, the child may be able to come up with his own solutions. Even when a parent is sure that he knows the answer—the child may have stolen something from the market when his mother was otherwise preoccupied; he may have broken undetected some family possession; he may have struck one of his friends—he may find that the most effective way to communicate the answer is to ask questions. This gives the child practice in formulating some basic moral and ethical principles, and it helps to do so in concert with adults he loves and trusts.

Dependence and Independence

All babies, if they are to develop well, need lavish amounts of affection and attention, which are really two ways of saying the same thing. The need for loving attention is as fundamentally organic as the need for food and shelter, and it must be satisfied. What happens in the absence of attention is shown by children raised in inadequately staffed orphanages and foundling homes. Babies in such institutions begin by crying for prolonged periods. After a while, crying gives way to apathy. The child becomes emotionally blunted and is likely to be below average in physical, motor, linguistic, and intellectual development.

Babies reared at home, but given insufficient attention, show the same effects in lesser degree. These observations should not be hard to understand. Babies have little in the way of inner resources. Their early psychological life is lived in interaction with concrete objects. They especially need contact with objects that respond and stimulate them to respond, like other human beings. Bonds of affection grow between the baby and the people with whom he interacts, and it is these bonds that make possible many positive developments: communication, discipline, social learning, intellectual learning, and, eventually, some level of independence.

Spoiling

Many parents, nonetheless, fear to pour out on the child the full measure of their love for fear that they will "spoil" the baby. As Spock has pointed out, it is impossible to spoil a baby by giving him too much loving attention. Bear in mind, of course, that as the baby gets older, loving attention has to be mixed in with a certain amount of control. Beyond age three months, for instance, when the baby begins fighting evening bedtime, bedtime is an unfavorable occasion for unstinting attention.

There are parents who spoil babies, but not by fulfilling the need for love and attention. This need, like the need to suck, gets satiated and becomes less intense when it is gratified. The spoiling parent may move in too fast every time the baby gives signs of discomfort, before either parent or baby has had time to find out what, if anything, is called for. In this way, parents may gratify the wrong need, leaving the baby with an ill-defined dissatisfaction that can lead to increased clamors for attention—or spoiling, if you will. At later ages, this kind of parental overresponsiveness can interfere with the development of language and problem-solving skills, and with the satisfaction the child takes in being able to do things for himself. There are also parents who try to compensate for a lack of genuine feeling by smothering the baby with unwanted or inappropriate attention. If needs are met inconsistently, the baby is left unsatisfied and perpetually demanding more.

In sum, the baby doesn't have an insatiable need for loving attention, and you don't have to worry about "giving in to him" too much. When his need for attention is fulfilled, the baby can turn toward other sources of stimulation and satisfaction besides his parents. Instead of spoiling him, loving attention helps him become independent.

Independence and Autonomy

Parents, I have said, want their children to be independent, but when you press parents to be more precise, it often turns out that they want a particular kind of independence and are much less enthusiastic about another. The kind of independence most parents prize is the kind that enables the child not to be a burden or bother to other people. That is, he should learn early to fend for himself, not to cling, to find his own amusements, to feed himself, dress himself, pick up his playthings, and all the rest.

The kind of independence that parents are likely to feel somewhat ambivalent about goes by the name of autonomy, the ability not only to take care of oneself but also to think and decide for oneself. The first kind of independence means getting along with a minimum of adult help, whereas autonomy may mean getting along with a minimum of adult authority and guidance.

As we have seen, the well-loved infant develops basic trust in his parents, in himself, and to some extent in the world in general. The trustful infant becomes the autonomous toddler who, now that he can walk and is beginning to talk, wants to do things for himself, without help or hindrance from others. The battle cries of the toddler struggling for autonomy are "Me!" and "No!" "Me!" means I want to do it myself, and "No!" means you can't make me. The toddler wants to feed himself at his own pace, dress himself, and not be told either to do or not to do something whether or not it is beyond his competence. In fact, toddlerhood sees the emergence of certain competences in American society. It is during this period that the child becomes able to eat with a spoon, drink from a glass that he himself holds, ride a tricycle, drink through a straw, chew gum without swallowing it, manage an ice cream cone, walk backward, run, hop, stand on one foot, and control elimination. There are, of course, numerous other things he cannot do, but except for truly dangerous undertakings, he has to be allowed to try.

Autonomy and Negativism

Autonomy, as we have seen, has two faces: the constructive one that pushes the child to mastery; and negativism, his strong resistance to adult control. Negativism is expressed in several ways—obviously, by saying no, and also by pulling away from the adult, or going stiff all over, or going limp all over, or erupting into tantrums. Just the interrogatory tone involved in asking the child a simple question may be enough to call forth a loud "No!"

Negativism sounds like a very disagreeable set of manifestations, but there is more to it than meets the superficial eye. First of all, we have to recognize its constructive functions, that it is part and parcel of the child's striving for competence. If the child insists on trying something for himself, such as winding up a toy car, and finds that he cannot manage, he simply turns the job over to the adult. What is more, if the parent can stay calm in the face of a barrage of no's, he may find that the child doesn't really mean it and keeps right on cooperating through a stream of verbal resistance. What is more, if

126

you look closely, you can see that many times the child is saying no in a spirit of play, as a form of teasing. He does not expect to be taken seriously and is shocked if he is.

Every so often, of course, the toddler means his negativism with every fiber of his being. Distraction may help, but sometimes there comes a show of wills. At such times, parental authority must prevail, but it doesn't have to explode. When the baby has a tantrum, adult calm is even more in order.

Growth Ambivalence

Now that we have portrayed the toddler as a monument of autonomy, we have to take back some of what we've said. For the toddler, like the rest of us, is always caught between two forces. One pushes him toward growth, mastery, exploration, and venturing into the unknown. The other holds him back, telling him to play it safe, preserve the status quo, and avoid the perils of growth. This conflict, called growth ambivalence, was expressed by one boy on his third birthday when he proclaimed tearfully, "I don't want to be three! I like being two!" The child Stuart, whose musings on life are extensively quoted in *Childhood and Adolescence,* put it this way: "Being big is the best, best thing, isn't it? . . . But sometimes I wish I didn't have to grow big. NOW! That's why you must take care of me and we will pretend I'm a little baby and have a long time to wait till I grow big." Growth ambivalence applies even in adulthood; if somebody offers us exactly the job we have been dreaming of, which promises all kinds of opportunities for freedom and initiative, we are likely to quail and tremble and hold back and have doubts.

The toddler alternates between clinging, babyish timidity and headlong sorties into new experience. He may start boldly down a ramp, then pause and reach out for an adult finger to help inch his way down. Incidentally, you should appreciate the power of a finger. Touch your forefinger to the toddler's hand, and almost invariably he will clasp it. He can then be guided almost at will, without forcing. Another time, the toddler, out on a walk, may decide to detour around a clump of bushes, with the seeming aim of rejoining the parent farther along. As soon as he loses sight of the adult, though, the erstwhile venturesome toddler panics and breaks into tears. There is nothing to be done about growth ambivalence except to recognize it, tolerate it, and lend the toddler your finger to get him over the rough spots. Being in contact with you soon restores his confidence, and he is ready to sally forth once more. His urge to autonomy needs no special encouragement.

Dual Ambivalence

Pushing the baby or young child into premature independence can backfire. But there is a contrary problem, that of holding him back, overprotecting him and retarding the development of competences and feelings of competence. There seem to be two main ways this happens. First, parents are liable to hover over the child, ready to protect him from his limited skill and poor judgment. Not to do so requires an act of will. Most of the time, the youngster cannot do himself or the environment much harm, and he is already protected against many dangers by parental taboos and by the conservative side of his own growth ambivalence.

The young child has to be watched, but unobtrusively. Parents should restrict their hovering to those few occasions when there is a real danger. Otherwise, the child should be free to try things out and make a few mistakes. He will invoke parental help quickly enough if he finds that he needs it. On those occasions when the child has to be protected, protection can be given without unduly restricting him. For instance, if there is danger that he may fall, a lightly encircling arm keeps him from harm without confining his movement.

The second way in which parents can retard their child's growth is more subtle. Parents obviously rejoice in every new accomplishment—the baby's first smile, the first time he rolls over, his first steps, his first word. Beginning very early, though, the thrill of passing a landmark is tempered by vague misgivings, which, in their child's toddlerhood, may find expression as "I'm losing my baby!" What this says is that parents share the baby's own growth ambivalence, that much as they want him to move toward independence, they also feel a sense of loss, of uncertainty, of everything happening too fast. The shared growth ambivalence of child and parent has been called dual ambivalence, which in practice often means that when the child is ready to move forward, the parents hold him back, and when the child wants to hold back, the parents press him ahead. The result can be considerable unnecessary friction. In general, except when the child is trying to do something wholly unsuitable, one takes one's cues from his impulses, letting him set the pace. The temptation to keep him a baby, to infantilize him, is strong and has to be resisted.

I mention only in passing that fathers and mothers may have quite different patterns of growth ambivalence about their children, the father pushing, being permissive, or retarding in some areas, while the mother does likewise in still others. I can remember from my own childhood the time my father took me to get a short haircut, which in those ancient days was the mark of being a "big" boy, and for which I had been clamoring for some time. When we got home, my mother wept with dismay at the sight of her shorn lambkin, and in my perhaps distorted recollection spent several days alternately lamenting the loss of my innocence and upbraiding my father for making it happen.

Dual ambivalence reaches a climax when the child grows to adolescence and is preparing, ambivalently, for the ultimate step into independence. But it begins early and can move parents to an unwitting but no less serious sabotage of development.

Separation

Sooner or later, parents have to turn over some part of the care of their child to other people—baby-sitters, grandparents, housekeepers, nurses, day care centers, preschools, schools. Sometimes a child has to go to the hospital, and sometimes a parent does. Each such separation carries with it two difficulties. First, the child misses his parents; normally, he forms strong, specific attachments to his father and mother, and in their absence he feels bereaved. Second, he has to learn to feel comfortable with new people and, perhaps, new surroundings—the same old problem of stranger anxiety.

It bears repeating that parents have a right and a need to escape from their children at times. Uninterrupted parenthood is bad for you. Both parents may work, which means that the child has to be looked after by somebody else. Some communes, of course, and some circles of parents who live near each other rotate the responsibility for taking care of the children. This may become a more widespread pattern but for the time being, most parents have to use more conventional ways of escape.

Let us see what can be done to minimize the strains of separation. The key to a stress-free transfer to supplementary caretakers is the same as for many other shifts: gradualism. Assuming that you have found a caretaker who meets your standards, do not be in a rush. If the child is going to be cared for at home, let the new person and this child get to know each other while one of you is around. For a time let the caretaker share with you in both looking after the child and handling incidental household duties. You will be able to tell when and if child and caretaker have found a common wavelength.

Sometimes, of course, you find that the caretaker you have chosen, no matter how well qualified, simply is not right for you and the child, and then you have no alternative but to start over. If caretaker and child do hit it off, gradually fade yourself out of the picture. Run some errands, visit a friend, take in a movie, go to work for a few hours. Watch for cues on your return. If the child greets you casually or cheerfully, things are going well. If he seems cool or distant or resentful, he may be punishing you for what feels to him like desertion. This means that you are hurrying the process and should make it more gradual.

Exactly the same procedures apply in reverse if the child is going to be taken care of outside the home. Go with him, stay with him, and slowly fade away. If the day care center or preschool is unwilling to cooperate in a gradual separation, think again. They may not know as much about children as they should. The story is different, of course, at later ages when the child goes off to kindergarten or first grade. Then he is old enough to know in advance that he will be on his own; he can be told about coming to terms with a group of children his own age and a new adult; and it can be taken for granted that a parent will not be hanging around to solace him. It is true that some parents are unwilling to let go—one teacher tells how she had to pull down the shades to thwart a mother who wanted to keep tabs on her child—but most know that this degree of separation is manageable for the school-age child.

There is, though, a hidden issue in relying on parental substitutes. It was brought home most forcefully by a pair of doctors who consulted me. They both worked long hours, he as a resident and she as an intern, and they had a full-time, live-in housekeeper-nursemaid. They were startled to find that their child seemed more attached to the housekeeper than to them, that in fact the child's beginning speech had the housekeeper's accents, and in general it appeared that the child was well along toward forming an identification with the housekeeper rather than the parents. My advice—I don't know whether they followed it—was that one or both would have to slow down the pursuit of a career to spend more time with the child and allow him to shift his primary attachment back to them.

The Lifelong Nature of Dependence

To put all this in perspective, no normal person ever outgrows all his dependent needs. Throughout life we need friends, mates, advisers; some people even become emotionally dependent on their children. We recognize as odd the person who seems totally self-sufficient, who seems to need no contact with his fellows. The rest of us need a certain amount of petting, fondling, soothing, hugging, reassurance, and support. Most of us need, in addition, admiration, praise, and the sense that we are Somebody. Children, of course, need it even more than we do.

It is also worth remembering that our pattern of attachments keeps shifting throughout life, that we outgrow people, ideas, and institutions even as we become fond of new ones. Parenthood begins with the cultivation of bonds and then, before we know it, there begins the slow, excruciating process of letting go, so that at some point our children will be able to walk out of our lives and into lives of their own. Not all parents can face up to this painful fact, but effective parenthood means pouring out vast quantities of emotion and energy which children should feel no obligation to repay. Our satisfaction has to be intrinsic—knowing we have raised strong human beings who no longer need parents to look after them.

6. SEX DIFFERENCES

With the growth of the Women's Liberation Movement, a person, especially a male person, takes his life in his hands when he talks about psychological differences between the sexes. Let me therefore be explicit: I am not preaching that anatomy is destiny. But all vertebrate animals, including humans, have two main biological sexes, with certain obvious contrasts of anatomy and physiology. The physiological contrasts include not only the workings of the reproductive apparatus but also hormonal differences which may affect brain function. Males are said to have a lower threshold for aggression than females, although this varies in poorly understood ways with how active the individual is sexually. Many females experience changes of mood in connection with their menstrual cycles, and lactating females of a number of species show more maternal behavior than males or non-lactating females (which, in the case of the golden hamster, are more likely to eat young pups than mother them).

These few observations tell us very little about a great many broader issues such as intellectual abilities, tastes and preferences, attitudes and beliefs, career choices and capabilities, interpersonal relations, parental roles, and life styles in general. The male and female roles have taken such different forms from era to era and from one society to the next that it is all but impossible to sort out what is cultural and what is biological.

Sex roles have three major components: sexual and

reproductive behavior; the functions assigned to each sex, together with rationalizations about each sex's special fitness or unfitness to perform various functions; and the "personality" traits that are assumed to go with being male or female.

All societies that have survived include among their sexual practices one or more that culminate in the discharge of semen into the vagina. Otherwise, a society lasts exactly one generation, like the Shakers and other celibate utopian communities. Beyond this *sine qua non,* diversity is the rule. The number of ways in which males and females can couple is wondrously varied. Both male and female homosexuality permit diverse expressions. Heterosexual and homosexual matings with animals also take different forms. Alexander Portnoy has described only some of the possible variations on the theme of autoerotism. Different cultures acknowledge and more or less openly countenance different ranges of sexual expression. Some practices are taboo, and the taboos are violated in varying degrees. There may even be culturally accepted forms for breaking taboos, as in the conventions that govern extramarital sex in the American middle class. One long-accepted principle of sexual conduct, now being challenged by Women's Liberation, is the double standard, which grants to men greater freedom of sexual exploration than to women.

A second theme of Liberation is the destruction of functional and occupational stereotypes, especially the assumption that women are by nature best suited to the homemaker role, or that when they work, are most appropriately cast in the roles of teacher, nurse, sales clerk, and secretary, whereas it is assumed that men naturally do best as intellectual and economic achievers. There is an irony here, in that women are clamoring for a greater role in business and the professions at the moment when large numbers of men are deciding that the usual patterns of striving in these fields are deluded and destructive. Some men are even proposing an inverted, cynical ninth beatitude: the female of the species shall inherit the pressures, the competition, the ulcers, the hypertension, and the lesser life expectancy.

Finally, there are all the traits supposedly associated with maleness and femaleness, beginning with "Snips and snails" and "Sugar and spice." Little girls are viewed as sweet, gentle, docile, volatile, sensitive, prone to tears, devious, and manipulating. It is assumed that the female is intrinsically dependent and will find fulfillment and identity only when she attaches herself to a male, bearing his children and in turn supporting his masculine identity. Boys are assumed to be tough, rambunctious, noisy, smart (but not scholarly), emotionally stable, assertive, combative, and protective of the weak and helpless (especially female). Maternal instincts and domesticity are supposed to blossom early in girls. Boys, by contrast, shun females except as sex objects, dodge family roles, and have to be domesticated and otherwise socialized by the wily female. Notice that our society is somewhat more tolerant of deviations from the female role than from the male: the girl can get away with being a tomboy, but there is nothing more damning than to be known as a sissy.

By the logic of the self-fulfilling prophecy, many males and females grow up acting as though their sex roles and traits had come to them via their genes. Others, however, do not. It is hard to know how contented those whose behavior fit the stereotypes are, but there is some reason to think that adhering to either sex role with great rigidity can be stressful. There is no doubt, however, about the psychic costs for those who violate the stereotype, particularly males. Just as the boy trembles at imputations of sissiness, so does the man quake at accusation of unmanliness.

One implication of our present stereotypes is that the sexes are cast as adversaries or even enemies, each trying to exploit the other at as little cost to itself as possible. No matter which side wins, it is a hollow victory. The prize is a beaten-down, washed-out member of the other sex who can no longer offer the victor any gratification.

One can blame the deterioration of marriage on either the punishment inflicted under the old codes or the fact that the codes are changing. It is possible that marriage in any form is a doomed institution, but it is also possible that a different view of marriage could produce some real and unique satisfactions. A number of proposals have been put forward: communal life with or without shared partners, open marriage, contractual marriage, marriage for a fixed term of years—I do not know all the options. I do believe, though, that a child needs at least two parents of different sexes. This belief would imply that those who want children should find some congenial form of marriage.

The war between the sexes undoubtedly plays a part in what looks like a sizable increase in homosexuality. Some part of the seeming increase, of course, is produced by long-time homosexuals "coming out of the closet" as public attitudes change. It is my impression that there is also an increase in the number of people, perhaps especially women, disenchanted with heterosexual relations who are looking for an alternative. It is not likely that many parents will deliberately raise their children to be homosexuals, but assuredly there will come a wider acceptance of homosexuality and homosexuals. It is not beyond imagining that bisexuality may someday be the dominant pattern, allowed for in future marital arrangements.

I have gone on at such length about these matters to try to convey that the teaching of sex roles nowadays involves conscious choices of a kind that did not arise when everybody "knew" what being a male or female meant. The role of learning, though, is no more absolute than the role of anatomy. There are always going to be sex differences, although they will probably be less pronounced and perhaps different in kind from the ones we know now. Our culture's definition of sex differences is in many ways arbitrary and even injurious. The best general policy is probably to concentrate on rearing good human beings, with a full range of intellectual and emotional resources, and let the biological influences work themselves out. In any case, worrying too much brings the self-fulfilling prophecy into play. If only for the record, however, we should say something more about both the biology and the psychology of sex differences.

The Biology of Maleness and Femaleness

In thinking about biological sex differences, we have to bear in mind that we all begin prenatally as females. Some of us stay that way, whereas others go through a further metamorphosis and become males. The basic difference is that those who become males have a Y chromosome, while those who stay female do not. Like several other chromosome pairs, the human sex chromosomes can come in several out-of-the-ordinary combinations. In addition to the standard XX female pattern and the XY male, there occur XXX, XO, XXY, XYY, and others. Any combination that contains a Y produces some kind of male. I have to say "some kind" because, in fact, there are not only two distinct biological sexes but a number of intermediate gradations. These can be the result of either an abnormal set of chromosomes or an abnormal endocrine environment before birth. Those gonads whose cells contain Y chromosomes develop into testes, and it is the secretions of male hormones from the testes that govern the further development of male rather than female anatomy.

Little boys discover their genitals at an earlier age than do little girls, if only because the penis is easily visible and accessible. Also, the boy has periodic erections from birth on, which probably contributes to his sense of himself as male (although not necessarily masculine in the conventional sense). Both sexes are capable of genital sensations beginning in early infancy. In some societies babies are masturbated to keep them quiet, which indicates that early genital experience may be more soothing than arousing. By late infancy, however, the expression on the face of a baby fondling his or her genitals tells us that genuine pleasure is involved.

Of course, the two sexes experience quite different sorts of puberty. Girls reach puberty at an earlier age than boys, and the age at puberty for both sexes is going down. Good nutrition and health accelerate puberty; living at high altitudes retards it—girls in Denver menstruate later, on the average, than girls in San Francisco. Both sexes grow rapidly as they approach puberty, both develop pubic and armpit hair, and both go through a change of voice, although this is more pronounced in boys than in girls. Girls develop bosoms and, at the point of puberty, begin to menstruate. (The first menstrual flow is called the menarche, pronounced men-ar'-key.) Boys develop facial hair, and the penis and scrotum enlarge and become pendulous. The boy has many spontaneous erections, which are accompanied by strong urges to ejaculate. He is likely to have nocturnal emissions—ejaculation during sleep—often in concert with erotic dreams. Moreover, the male can be aroused to erection and lust by a great many sights, sounds, odors, ideas—it can be said that many adolescent boys inhabit a libidinized environment, in which almost everything has sexual significance. The case with girls is less clear. Kinsey's perhaps obsolete data indicate that girls are less easily aroused than boys. It seems clear that girls have become more active sexually than they were in Kinsey's day, but we need another Kinsey to find out what their experience feels like to them. Some people feel that the lower arousability reported by Kinsey was caused by the greater repressiveness of our society's attitudes to female sexuality. This could mean either that sexuality was stifled, that sex was given disagreeable connotations, or simply that girls received less sexual stimulation than boys. Female sexuality may be changing as our mores change, but the occasional confidences I receive from college students suggest that the change is not all that rapid, and that a great many young women are hurting from peer pressure to become sexually active.

Teaching and Learning Sex Roles

There is no denying the potency of social influences on the development of sexual identity. Whatever parents may think about the proper roles for boys and girls, they should be aware of the numerous and often subtle ways in which these roles get communicated.

A major component in psychological development is identification, or taking on the ways of the people to whom the child is exposed. Identification goes much deeper than behavior, of course. It involves coming to think and feel the way familiar people do. Identification in early childhood is seldom if ever a conscious, rational, deliberate process. For better or for worse, the child soaks up the styles, the mannerisms, the speech patterns, the attitudes and assumptions of the people surrounding him. These are primarily the father and mother, but older siblings, baby-sitters, and neighbors can all play a part.

As the child gets older, his world expands and the variety of people with whom he can identify multiplies: teachers, peers, public figures, entertainers and celebrities, fictional characters, whoever. In some sense, the child likewise identifies with his physical and geographical surroundings, familiar foodstuffs, institutions, and all that goes to make up the local culture.

During the middle years of childhood, through adolescence, and into adulthood, there is often a process of counteridentification at work, whereby the young person repudiates past identifications and tries to answer his own uniqueness. Here we have James Joyce rejecting his

Catholic upbringing but remaining inescapably Catholic in his style of thinking; the countless small-town young people who migrate to the cities, ostensibly in search of fame and fortune but more fundamentally looking for a new identity; and adolescent rebels shouting slogans of freedom from the identifications that haunt them and will not be shaken off.

An important part of identification is, of course, acquiring an identity as male or female. Some of the processes by which sex identification takes place are reasonably well known. It is said that girls identify with their mothers, whereas boys identify with a generalized male role. This statement has a grain of truth, but it is far from complete. For one thing, not all identification means being like others. One learns both to be like members of one's own sex and to find a way of relating to the opposite sex. It seems quite clear that a significant part of the girl's sexual identity arises from a sort of reciprocal identification with the father. Oedipus and Electra aside, many fathers provide so deep an image of masculinity that their daughters never recover from it. One might suspect that the fathers involved are not altogether unhappy about this outcome.

The cross-identification of little boys with their mothers seems less pronounced, although elements are certainly there, and there are plenty of Oedipuses around. If boys identify with a generalized masculinity, it is through the medium of their fathers. It is worth repeating that to have no father or an inadequate father is a most unfortunate circumstance for boys and girls alike. Recent findings by Hetherington and Deur suggest, however, that for girls the sex-role consequences of separation from the father may not show up until adolescence. Father-deprived girls showed extremes of either promiscuity or withdrawal from males.

Imitation

From an early age, children imitate the actions of other people. Imitation is something of a mystery: how is it possible that we translate a visual or auditory experience to a motor performance that reproduces what we have just seen or heard? Nobody knows, but one cannot deny the extent or importance of imitation. Kittens learn to catch mice by watching their mothers catch mice. Apes learn to solve problems by watching other apes solve them. (Here a complication enters, for apes learn faster from another ape's mistakes than from his successes.) Babies copy all kinds of actions, whether they understand them or not. Imitating people seems to contribute powerfully to feeling at one with them and making their ways one's own.

Modeling

Modeling is akin to imitation, but it refers not to copying particular acts but rather to taking over whole styles of acting from another person who serves as a model. With respect to physical violence, the baby or young child seems to absorb whole orientations to the world from the behavior of significant people. So with sex roles. It is the essential style of masculinity that gets transmitted to the little boy, and that of femininity to the girl, as well as the special actions performed by male and female models. Thus, the two-year-old son of a swaggering father swaggers along at Daddy's side, the tiny daughter of a mincing mother minces for all she is worth.

As we know, children of both sexes model their behavior on the actions of other persons of both sexes, as is best illustrated by specific imitation: the little girl tries to smoke her father's pipe, the little boy goes through the motions of shaving his legs. Nevertheless, perhaps with the help of the other mechanisms we shall talk about, the role models get sorted out and the children pick up the "correct" masculine or feminine style.

Dramatic Play

Starting in toddlerhood, we can see the effects of imitation and modeling in dramatic play, the child's enactment of scenes based on everyday life. The toddler's dramatic play, sometimes called symbolic play, is at first simple and episodic. He "feeds" his dolls, wipes their noses, and puts them to bed. He engages in such activities as telephoning, having tea, shaving, and driving the car. He trails his mother about the house, "helping" with the housework.

During the preschool years, dramatic play becomes more elaborate as the child learns of the larger world of construction projects, the supermarket, and complex human relationships. The cops and robbers and cowboys and Indians of the school-age child are recurring themes of dramatic play. In some times and places, the violent games of schoolchildren shade into actual violence, as is happening currently in Northern Ireland.

Older preschool children and younger school kids may act out fairy tales, television commercials, circuses, or invented skits. Athough the child has no inkling of it, his pretending to be pilot, housewife, bulldozer operator, mechanic, librarian, father, mother, doctor, whatever, introduces him to the adult world and helps shape his vision of life. Sometimes, of course, the child's dramatic play mirrors back our own style of life in ways that are less than flattering. It may be only when we hear our child "telephoning" that we realize how affected a voice we use on the phone; the scoldings the child addresses to his dolls may reveal some of our own harshness. Thus, the child's play may be educational for his parents as well as himself. In any event, his acting out the roles of male and/or female helps define for him these two states of being.

Reinforcement and Shaping

Edward Thorndike gave us the concept of instrumental learning, popularized by B. F. Skinner, which says that we learn from the consequences of our actions. A parent or teacher is often in a position to control the consequences of a child's behavior, and so to shape it in desired directions. The traditional view of consequences is as reinforcers, which may be positive or rewarding; or neutral, which means in effect no consequences; or negative or aversive or punishing.

A more up-to-date view is that consequences provide feedback, on the analogy of a computer that performs an operation and then, on the basis of the results of that operation, "knows" what to do next. A homely analogy is a game of twenty questions, where we are "fed" one piece of information, which takes us to the next logical step. In everyday life feedback comes so thick and fast that we generally take no conscious notice of it. The doorknob tells the hand when to stop turning without our having to think about it, the stair treads tell the feet to stop descending, the food in the mouth tells us when to remove the fork and start chewing. It is only under adverse conditions we become aware of feedback: groping our way in the dark, walking over rocky terrain or in soft sand, trying to figure out a new gadget. The play of expression on the face of the person we are talking to tells us that we are boring him stiff, or wounding his feelings, or entertaining him, or violating his code of propriety. When we are cut off from normal feedback, as when we try to put our weight on a foot that has gone to sleep, our behavior disintegrates.

Parents, whether they know it or not, are forever giving the child subtle cues to whether he is acting appropriately. It is not only the overt approbations—"How lovely you look in your new dress," "That's the big boy" —and disapprobations—"That's not ladylike," "Boys don't act that way"—that shape us in the desired ways, but also the signs of strain, embarrassment, pride, shame, or whatever. Just as the adult may be unaware of providing feedback, the child may be unaware of receiving and responding to it. Thus, the taking on of sex roles may seem to all involved the simple fulfilling of a biological design rather than a study in operant conditioning. One way or another, children get society's message: take as your model members of your own sex.

Later, when the child moves out of the family circle into the play group or nursery school, new adults as well as his playmates will continue the process of sex-role shaping, with the pressures becoming more intense with increasing age. As I have said, the sanctions are more severe for the sissy than the tomboy, but adherence to the standard roles wins the child acceptance or praise, and deviation brings rebukes, scorn, and ridicule.

Parental Handling

The very ways in which parents pick up, hold, talk to, play with, and feed the baby help tell him whether he or she is male or female. Even in the newborn nursery the skilled observer can tell from a mother's behavior with her child whether it is a girl or a boy.

You can probably fill in from imagination some of the differences in the ways the two sexes are handled. Girls are treated as fragile, boys as sturdy. Though it seems unlikely, repeated observation has shown that the girl baby's crying gets reacted to faster than the boy baby's. Mothers touch their baby daughters more often than they do their infant sons, and they talk to them more. Since these differences in handling begin at the very beginning of postnatal life, there seems to be no point where we can measure pure, natural sex differences uncontaminated by experience. It is only lately that psychologists have begun to study the characteristics of *babies* as these affect parental behavior, but one of the first characteristics to be studied was sex, and it has been seen to make a difference. You can sense the difference by imagining that the obstetrician refused to tell you whether the baby was a boy or a girl.

Sex-Typed Playthings and Activities

We take for granted that there are clear-cut differences between the sexes in the kinds of toys they like to play with and the sorts of games they enjoy. Girls are given miniature versions of household articles, dolls, nurse's kits, and the like, and are encouraged to act out domestic roles. Boys are given sports equipment, trucks and cars, building blocks, and other replicas from the extra-domestic arena, and are expected to act out themes of combat, adventure, and accomplishment. Girls learn to jump rope, play jacks and hopscotch, read cozy, romantic books, and dress up as adults. Boys learn not only to ride bikes but to take them apart and put them together, to explore woods and seashore, to fish and hunt, to camp out, to play baseball, football, and basketball, and in general to enact the he-man role. There is no formal research telling us how early differential access to playthings and instruction in sex-typed activities has an effect in shaping masculine and feminine world-views, but everyday observation suggests that the process is well advanced by age three.

Parents who are inclined to let children work out their own patterns of tastes and preferences would probably do well to bias the playthings they provide to children of *both* sexes in a masculine direction. It requires little thought to realize that the experience of little girls is deprived as compared to that of little boys, with one exception. Beyond the preschool years, when children are reading on their own, there is an abundance of good books for girls, and comparatively little for boys. I make the differentiation in terms of whether the main character is male or female, and not in terms of the events portrayed; the simple fact is that boys do not enjoy reading books with heroines rather than heroes, although girls accept male protagonists. For preschool children, happily, there is an excellent unisex literature. (I might remark in passing that most parents need to learn how to read to small children—clearly, at a leisurely pace, and with expression.)

Although the choice of playthings for children should in general have a male bias, little boys should have dolls, stuffed animals, and materials for domestic play, however dismaying parents may find the idea. There is nothing in the male constitution that forbids playing parent, expressing tenderness and compassion, and in general enjoying many of the same things as girls. For instance, boys as well as girls enjoy skipping rope, but they are restrained from doing so by some cryptic taboo built into the culture. Many parents act as though they think that playing girls' games will undermine a boy's virility and turn him into a sissy or a homosexual. I would suggest, on the contrary, that the many sexual difficulties reported for American males are related to their not having had a chance as small children to practice a wide range of feelings. Observers of the American scene feel that latent homosexuality is rampant, and are more than ready to point the finger of suspicion at those who most flamboyantly play the role of hypermasculinity (certain macho authors come readily to mind). The central principle is to let little boys and girls find out for themseves how best to define their own sex roles.

Instruction and Indoctrination

The things we have talked about so far—imitation, modeling, dramatic play, reinforcement and feedback, handling, and the provision of playthings and activities—have all been the subject of psychological research, some of it very ingenious. However, the psychologists have neglected one rather obvious mechanism for transmitting sex roles and rules: telling the child how or—more often—how not to behave. A recurring refrain in communication from parent to child is "Girls don't do that" or "Boys don't do that" or "That's not for girls" or, more specifically, "Boys don't cry" or "That's not ladylike." Thus, in addition to instructing boys and girls in different kinds of activities, adults often make explicit the rules of conduct for the two sexes. These rules are by no means coherent and consistent: the boy is expected to be simultaneously Little Lord Fauntleroy and Tom Sawyer, the girl both pure and alluring.

As we can see, the child is on the receiving end of countless messages defining his or her sex role. This state of affairs will continue for some time to come. We are always aware of changes that take place in the more visible segments of society—Sexual Revolution, Black Revolution, the Student Movement, Women's Liberation —and tend to conclude that the values of society as a whole are in a ferment. In fact, cultural change in the large mass of people goes on at a glacial pace.

If you want to raise children free of the sex-role stereotypes of past generations, you should do so in full expectation that the liberated child will often be at odds with his peers and their families. He may even suffer ostracism, which is nothing less than capital punishment for children. There is a serious ethical dilemma here. For our children's own sake, we want to bring them up in the best light of modern reason; at the same time, we recognize that we have no right to use our offspring as instruments of the social change we wish to effect. The best, somewhat lame answer I have to offer is that we raise our children as we see fit within humane bounds, but that we be prepared to tell children that many others feel differently about things and they will have to learn to live peacefully with persons of quite different persuasions. In any case, I may be too pessimistic; there are indicators of change at the grass-roots level, too. It is just possible that the silent majority has been doing some private soul-searching and decided that social change is in order. I still see all about me little boys and girls being socialized for traditional roles, but like the accumulated black resentments that boiled forth in the 1950s and 1960s, female resentment of second-class citizenship is bound to spread and become a major social force.

7. EARLY SEXUALITY

Sex roles are related, if irregularly, to the biology of reproduction. Human beings have learned to exploit their reproductive functions as self-contained activities, for pleasure divorced from procreation. Thus, like sex roles, human sexuality is only incidentally related to having progeny.

For long centuries it was taken for granted in Western societies that sexuality began at puberty, when the sexual apparatus matures. Precocious manifestations were ignored, belittled, or punished as marks of depravity. The Sigmund Freud gang changed all that. Freud opened people's reluctant eyes to the pervasiveness of sex in human experience. He further insisted that sex is a lifelong phenomenon, not restricted to biological adulthood but, as we have seen, beginning in infancy. Freud made the point that sex wears countless disguises, so that we can be behaving sexually when engaged in activities superficially without any sexual connotations. Much of psychopathology was to be understood as the product of sexual misfortunes early in life. Freud gave us the notion of the Oedipus complex and its female counterpart, the Electra complex. He never worked out the details of the Electra complex to his own satisfaction, and many women's liberationists are unhappy with the Freudian account of female psychosexual development, including the notions of penis envy and the castrating woman, and Freud's failure to endow women with a capacity for ethical and moral judgments.

It is worth taking a moment to clear up a couple of common misconceptions. Never did Freud advocate sexual license. He believed in the inheritance of acquired characteristics, and he saw the suppression and redirection of instincts by society as a necessary part of human evolution. People became so preoccupied with Freud's views on eroticism that they tend to neglect the other major component of human motivation set forth by Freud —the death wish. Lorenz's current theory of a human instinct to aggression is a direct echo of Freud's thinking.

Freud initiated a revolution in thinking about human behavior, and we are in his debt for bringing sexuality into the open and for making us realize that we are often strangers to our own motives. As a theory of human nature, though, psychoanalysis will not stand up. Anthropologists and experimental psychologists have cast serious doubts about the concept of an instinct to destruction. It has come to be accepted that not all affection, compassion, and concern is a disguised representation of sexual lust. Intellectual curiosity and the mastery of intellectual and other skills are now viewed as satisfying in their own right, without appeals to hidden motives and devious reworkings. Most generally, the main theme in American psychology—that human nature is highly malleable and can take widely diverse forms according to childhood experience—has been largely vindicated, despite occasional eruptions of biological and genetic determinism. Determinism itself, the idea that we are passive products of either our biology or our experience, is gradually yielding to the view that human beings have at least some capacity for *self*-determination, for thinking through their situation in life and making reasoned, if seldom wholly rational, decisions.

Even though we do not have to buy the Freudian package entire, we do have to acknowledge that father–daughter and mother–son relations often have a special quality reminiscent of the Oedipus and Electra complexes. Both of the little girls whose early years are portrayed in

Three Babies show Electra-like leanings. Here is her mother's account of Deborah, not quite two years old:

> Apparently has decided she needs to see more of Daddy, so suddenly has decided to call for him to "Open door" at 7 A.M., wastes no time with diaper change, but proceeds to dog his heels, prompting him and imitating shaving and tooth-brushing, helping him dress (holds pant legs, gets shoes, helps with shoe horn, etc.) And now eats breakfast in his lap, with smug satisfaction, begrudging him every single bite, and flirting with him. . . . In the evening, greetings are nonchalant until he is settled, and then she monopolizes him in all sorts of activity, after telling Mommy to "Go way."

And here is Ruth, not quite twenty-two months old:

> Ruth shows signs of jealousy. Whenever I kiss her father, she runs to him and says, "My daddy."

At twenty-three months, Ruth's mother reports:

> [We] were having dinner in the dining room, and I went into the kitchen for something. I returned and Ruth said resentfully, "Mommy go in the kitchen. Ruthie and her husband are eating. Mommy don't sit with us."

A number of babies make it a practice to climb into bed with their parents, often with a view to hugging and snuggling with the opposite-sex parent. Fathers and mothers are ambivalent about this practice. It can be especially embarrassing if Father, hugging his little girl, has a sudden erection.

In general, I would advise against allowing the baby into the parental bed. Once in a while as a special treat, perhaps, but certainly not as a regular thing. Most parents want privacy and should learn to lock their bedroom door.

The Child's Discovery of His Body

We should note at the beginning that self-knowledge develops in various degrees in different individuals. This, of course, is fully compatible with Freudian thought. Some people have very little sense of themselves as thinking, choosing, controlling agents in their own behavior. In studies of what has come to be known as locus of control, some subjects consistently assign blame for their failures and credit for their successes to external forces: luck, the supernatural, or unspecified "pressures." One psychologist, Julian Jaynes, dates the dawn of human consciousness from the time, about 800 B.C., that people began to realize that they talk to themselves and that the voices they perceive figuring out courses of action are their own, and not those of gods, demons, and other spirit forces. The hallucinations of both normal people and schizophrenics seem to result from the interpretation of internal experience as external. But more usually, we learn, slowly, to draw a sometimes blurred boundary between self and world, beginning with our own bodies.

When we watch babies carefully, we can see two lines of development with respect to body awareness. First, the baby gains command of different parts of his body, and second, he discovers parts of his body as objects of attention and exploration and testing. He comes to know his body both as a concrete instrument for dealing with the world and as its own object, something to be experienced in itself.

In terms of competences, the baby comes into the world with eyes, ears, nose, and mouth in good working order. All these are sense organs, but the mouth in addition is a prehensile tool, something with which to grasp and hold on and manipulate. For all practical purposes, it is the baby's only prehensile tool for the first couple of months after birth. His hands are of little use to him. If you stimulate the fingers of a newborn's closed fist with your own finger, he will open his hand and grasp the stimulating finger, in many cases with such force that he can support his own weight. Very soon after birth he begins to clasp the breast or bottle while being fed. Some babies can suck their thumbs immediately after birth, while others are able only with great effort to hook their fingers into the mouth. That is the extent of the manual repertory at birth. During the child's infancy, you can watch the baby gaining control: of his head, so that he can turn it to look and listen; of his hands, so that he can swipe at dangling objects and then grasp them; of his whole body, so that he can roll over, sit up, crawl on his belly, get up on all fours, and creep; of his feet, as assistant hands and then as members to stand and walk on.

You can also observe a parallel set of discoveries. The baby watches fascinated as his hand twists and his fingers waggle before his eyes. He finds his feet, captures them, and drags them to where he can look at them and fit them into his mouth. Late in infancy, as we have seen, the baby explores parental facial features and then palpates his own corresponding ones; by this age he already knows himself in the mirror (I do not know if the same pattern of discovery happens in mirrorless societies). The baby discovers his navel, poking it and working the skin around to watch its variations in shape. The little boy, typically in his bath and usually at about age one, one day notices an odd bit of flesh in the water and grabs it; his smirk of pleasure contains an element of surprise that tells us that he did not anticipate this result. The little girl's discovery of her vulva comes later, whether through a random exploration of unseen regions or an exploration guided by local sensation. In any case, once the baby has found this treasured bit of anatomy, he or she returns to it often to sample its pleasures.

The baby's experience of his body, both as an instrument of action and as an object for scrutiny and manipulation, gradually gets knitted into an overall schema that gives him a continuing sense of his body as a whole. There are two kinds of evidence for intermediate stages in the development of a body schema. The toddler obviously needs some degree of whole-body coordination to walk and trot and hop, but he fails the test of knowing without seeing it whether you are poking his skin with a single finger or with two fingers inches apart, even though he readily distinguishes single things and double things visually. Similarly, if he suffers a wound such as a fly bite, he may not be able to tell you where it hurts—pediatricians know better than to ask a young child to tell where something hurts. A couple of phenomena observable in adults show how much more strongly developed the body schema becomes. The experience of trying to stand on a foot that has gone to sleep indicates that the foot remained as part of one's experienced body even though it had lost its sensitivity to outside stimulation. One feels the numbness and tingling of a "sleeping" extremity only when the nerve resumes functioning. The second phenomenon is that of the phantom limb, the member that feels as though it is still there even though it has been amputated—one can even feel pain in a phantom limb. Children born with an arm or leg missing never experience phantoms for these absent members, indicating that the body schema is not laid down in the nervous system but has to be acquired through active, passive, and self-stimulated experience.

Awareness of one's own body is never complete. Indeed, since the body changes all through life, the body image must be revised from time to time. We also know that representation of the internal organs of the body is highly diffuse, even in persons with an advanced knowledge of anatomy, which makes it very easy for people to have bizarre delusions and hallucinations about their inner workings. One person I know, not a psychotic, complained that he had pockets of gas throughout his body.

Our sense of self transcends our body awareness— as in our scheme of values, our goals, our sense of competence, and other realms that are not clearly related to having a particular kind of human constitution. Nevertheless, our experience of our bodies—as beautiful or plain or ugly, as weak or strong, as big or little, as healthy or sickly, as sexually alive or inert—is a significant component in our total sense of identity.

Early Genital Experience

As we have seen, in many societies adults masturbate babies as a way of quieting them, and genital experience is apparently pleasantly soothing at first rather than lustfully arousing. By the end of infancy, though, genital stimulation clearly produces strong pleasure qualitatively different from other sensuous experience—eating, chewing, sucking, listening to music, being cuddled, whatever. But the intensified genital experience of late infancy seems to lack one ingredient of adult sexuality in that it does not appear to rise toward an orgasmic climax. This may be, of course, because babies do not know how to stimulate themselves fully.

Masters and Johnson report that adult techniques of self-stimulation are for the most part rather limited and unimaginative, and it seems unlikely that babies would do better. Kinsey records the behavior of a three-year-old girl who regularly masturbated to orgasm, but this seems to be an exceptional case. It suggests, however, that the capacity for female orgasm, given the right kinds of stimulation, appears quite early. On the other hand, in Kinsey's sample of the 1940s it appeared that most women achieved full sexual maturity only in their thirties, with the amount of experience being an important influence. Even though baby boys cannot ejaculate, they too might be capable of climax, but to the best of my knowledge this is, scientifically, unexplored territory.

Attitudes Toward Masturbation

Once the baby has discovered his or her genitals, as I have said, he or she returns to them for more of the same sensations. Infantile masturbation used to vie with thumb-sucking as a source of adult consternation. In one section of a child-care manual of the 1930s you could find advice that the baby should be put to bed with his hands under the covers to prevent thumb-sucking, and in another section, that his hands should be left outside the covers to prevent masturbation.

I hope that attitudes have changed. Despite the folklore, masturbation does not debilitate people, sexually or otherwise; it does not stunt growth or induce mental deficiency. Babies who get a lot of adult attention and have plenty of scope and playthings spend very little time in the land of Eros. Masturbation, like thumb-sucking, is most frequent at bedtime, when the baby is letting his ties to the outside world dissolve and is entering the world of somatic self-sufficiency. What I am saying is that there is ordinarily no reason to do anything about masturbation. If it becomes an all-consuming preoccupation for the child, it means that there are deficiencies in other areas of his life which have to be seen to. It is curious that in the midst of what was widespread cultural condemnation of masturbation—including the idea that it meant that the young man could not have access to real sex—Kinsey's research showed that almost all adolescent and adult males masturbated.

Without any particular adult intervention, the child of preschool age will get the idea that one does not masturbate in public. If necessary, he can even be told as much. One of the things that go with development of the body scheme is a sense of privacy about one's body—which obviously takes different forms in different cultural settings—and preschool children in our society seem to develop a spontaneous modesty. I recall bathing a little girl with whom I was baby-sitting. It suddenly dawned on her that there was something amiss about being naked in the presence of a strange man, so somewhat flustered, she placed her hands over her nipples. And there was the time when my daughter, seeing a painting of a nude, commented, "Isn't she embarrassed?"

Sexual Curiosity

Children learn about their own external anatomy by touching it and looking at it directly and in the mirror, but they are slow in generalizing what they know to other people. Children from an early age—certainly by age two—distinguish the two sexes quite reliably. Older research, however, showed that young children relied on hair styles and clothing rather than anatomy to tell them which was which. I remember one little girl happening on a photograph of a nude girl with close-cropped hair; she asked, "Why doesn't that boy have any clothes on?" Once the evidence of girlhood was shown her, she accepted it, but still somewhat skeptically. We need new research to tell us what the distinguishing cues of masculinity and femininity are for young children now that hair style or clothing is no longer a reliable guide.

Left to his own devices, the child is likely to form some anatomical misconceptions. I once overheard a little boy urging a little girl to show him her penis. When she denied having one, he retorted, "You must have. My mommy's got one." A little girl, asked what she hoped the sex of the new baby would be, answered, "A boy-girl. You know, a girl with a penis." One way to counteract the development of such misconceptions is to give the child ample occasion to learn about anatomy by observation. What this translates into practically is that parents allow the baby and young child to see them undressed as well as dressed. Many parents are aghast at the thought of appearing nude in front of their young children, and it seems pointless to urge them to shed their inhibitions. (I favor full disclosure, but parents have to obey their own feelings.) Others can be quite relaxed about having the creeping or toddling baby follow them about, watching as they use the toilet, bathe, groom themselves, and dress and undress. During menstruation, the mother is likely to practice privacy. As we suggested earlier, the baby or young child observes more than the parental anatomy, since he imitates the behavior of the adults. But he scrutinizes the adult bodies closely, sometimes asking questions and making comments. Parents will differ in the extent to which they can tolerate the baby's actually handling their private parts in the course of his investigations. If you're going to be embarrassed, don't do it. As the child approaches school age, most parents begin to cover themselves and keep the bathroom door shut.

Sooner or later the young child is going to want to know about where babies come from. Once again, one should err on the side of generosity in giving information. Much of what you tell the child will not register, but I assume that it is ignorance that is the breeding ground of the birth theories that children invent. When asked about the birth process, children propose that babies get out through the anus, or navel, or that the mother has to be cut open, and they expect the baby to come into the world smeared with feces or half-digested food from having been in the mother's "tummy" (euphemisms are a blight on communication, but they are particularly deadly when visited on children).

A student once told me that as an adolescent she had figured out that girls get pregnant from being close to a male during menstruation. During her period, she reported, she kept having to duck into doorways lest some passing male impregnate her. Another woman had been married some time before she found out that impregnation does not take place via the anus.

We cannot guarantee that answering questions about

the facts of life frankly is going to immunize the child
against wild hypotheses, but truthfulness seems preferable
to lies and evasions. The chief principle seems to be to tell
the child what he or she wants to know, and not push the
matter or be solemn about it. The child will be back in
his own good time with more questions. A friend of mine
tells how she gave her daughter the full treatment the
first time she asked about the origin of babies. At the
end, the daughter thought for a moment and said, "Tell
me one thing, Mommy. Do you have to take down your
panties?" My friend said it was some time before she
could again have intercourse.

From time immemorial, little boys and girls have been
saying, "I'll show you mine if you'll show me yours," and
more than one pair has followed through on the proposi-
tion, sometimes with some touching and pinching and
poking as well. In some societies, children act out sexual
intercourse, to the amusement of their elders, although it
is doubtful that the prepubertal boy ever achieves penetration. Such encounters, whether furtive or open, seem
to work no harm (sexual or otherwise) on children, and
should cause parents—if they find out about them—no
distress.

Incest and Seduction

Most parents can accept with equanimity a certain
amount of sex play with peers, which by definition cannot
proceed very far. More disturbing is the thought of an
adult or older child having sexual relations with a baby
or young child. One has to accept that babies can be
sexual stimuli, that adults can be aroused to desire by the
sight or smell or touch of an infant or toddler. This applies not only to family friends and in-laws and aunts and
uncles, but to the baby's immediate family—father and
mother and older sibs.

If incest taboos are strong, it may be because they

have to be. In a fair number of cases, the taboos are not strong enough and in the case of older brothers, incest taboos seem to be very little deterrent at all; in some corners of world society, it is said that the age of consent is the age at which the little girl first gets left alone with her older brother.

Homosexual incest with siblings is not unheard of. Father–daughter incest, starting when the little girl is an infant, may be, from what I have been able to learn, far from uncommon, bearing in mind that incest can stop short of vaginal penetration by the phallus. Incest fantasies, disguised or overt, are to be found in the fathers of many baby girls. James Joyce asserted that father–son incest was the one form unknown to humankind, but he was wrong, and Kinsey's files hold the cases to prove it. Mother–son incest seems to be less common than the father–daughter variety, whether because mothers are less easily turned on, or because the taboos have been laid down more strongly, or just because little boys are somewhat unreliable sexual partners. Quasi-sexual relations between mothers and their sons are so common as not to merit notice.

The matter becomes complicated because not only is the baby or small child a more powerful sexual stimulus than we like to admit, but the child may actively seduce the adult. Whether it is learned or innate, and whether the motivation is sexual or simply relates to the pleasure of having an effect on people, babies and young children often move their bodies in ways that are highly provocative, and their snugglings against the adult body have voluptuous overtones.

Thus, the molester of small children is not necessarily a depraved character who prowls about working evil on hapless victims. Probably in most cases the child molester is a relative or family friend who caved in to temptation. Most instances go undetected. While precocious sexual experiences should be avoided, it seems to leave very little mark on the child. Obviously, some children have highly traumatic early sexual experiences because of elements of coercion or violence, or because of something that leads the child to interpret the situation as cataclysmic, and the aftereffects can be very enduring. Most of the child's sexual encounters with adults, however, are little more serious than sex play with peers or with oneself. In general, of course, our sexual attitudes have been reversed. We used to worry about protecting the innocence and purity of young people, whereas now we worry that they may have inhibitions and hang-ups, or will not have sexual opportunities, or for whatever other reason will remain sexually unfulfilled. Relaxed sexual attitudes have their origin in the cradle.

In sum, then, tell your children what they want to know. Protect them against molestation, but if it happens, don't overact and inflate it into a doomsday event. Search your conscience and make sure your child has not somehow become tainted for you. Even though you think you are treating him normally, you may be unconsciously punishing him or treating him as something to be kept at arm's length. We are in the middle of a sexual revolution and the old rigidities will have to go, even though we lack a clear chart to the future.

8. LANGUAGE
AND COMMUNICATION

We have already seen, in Chapter 3, how the process of communication begins long before the baby can talk. Sensitive parents learn to respond to the baby's "language of behavior," the ways in which he expresses his needs. The baby further learns to communicate his desires by shrieking, pointing, and vocalizing and gesturing in other ways. Late in the first year, the baby comes to understand a certain amount of what is said to him in the form of commands, requests ("Please hand me my slippers"), and cue words for games and activities ("Peekaboo," "Bath time").

The baby's preverbal communication has its non-human animal counterparts. The baby's cries of hunger, pain or loneliness, his gurgles of contentment, and his laugh of delight are expressive behavior analogous to the mooing of the cows at sundown as they cluster at the pasture gate, or to the wagging of the dog's tail and the bristling of the cat's fur. The baby's shouts and gestures are equivalent to the dog's barking for attention, scratching at the door to be let out, and rolling over to have his belly scratched. Both dogs and babies communicate with tokens. The dog brings his food dish to ask for dinner, and his leash to be taken for a walk; the baby brings his coat to ask to be taken out, and brings a record to have it played.

Adults take it for granted that they can read the language of behavior of animals, yet profess bewilderment at the language of behavior of babies. In fact, if you understand the needs of babies, especially those that go beyond the physical into the realm of contact, affection, attention, play, and communication, the messages contained in behavior are quite simple to decipher. Even when you are unsure about what is called for, you can try likely satisfiers, and the feedback you get from the baby will tell you whether you are on the right track. Recently books have been published on the topic of "body language," offering to teach you how to interpret some of the nonverbal components of adult communication. No such book has been written about babies, but none is really needed.

Like babies, household pets learn a certain amount of passive language and respond appropriately to some words. But with respect to language, dogs and cats do not go beyond the immediately pragmatic. Babies, by contrast, get the more general idea of language itself. This awareness seems to begin, as it did with Helen Keller's rediscovery of language, with the realization that things have names. One form of preverbal communication that many parents fail to notice is the infant's asking for the names of things. Once the baby has begun speaking, his recurrent "Whadda?" reveals his hunger for words. But alert parents will find that even earlier the baby will point at something, look inquiringly at the adult, and make an interrogatory sound—the sound may be simply a grunt or a better-articulated "duh," but in either case you can hear the question mark at the end. If the adult supplies the name of the thing the baby is pointing to, the baby makes a sound of acknowledgment and goes on about his business. I suspect that for this kind of treatment the baby selects objects that are salient for him but that seldom get named. For instance, when preparing to bathe the baby, the adult is likely to say, "Let's turn on the water"; water is a familiar enough substance to the baby, but he is likely to become curious about the unnamed faucet, which both my children did. Similarly for the switch with which we "turn on the light."

If you agree with me that language is the ultimate humanizer, the raiser of the human being to full consciousness, the means by which people can dwell and function in abstract and remote and imaginary realms, you will understand the importance of cultivating the child's linguistic abilities to the full. I have argued this position in my book *Language and the Discovery of Reality*. Here I shall only assert it.

The cultivation of language takes several forms. One is the encouragement of the baby's babbling, most usually by babbling back at him both in imitation of the forms he uses and in nonsense words beyond his immediate capacities. Babbled "conversations" between adult and child usually begin at age three or four months, when the baby can make some spontaneous sounds besides crying, sneezing, hiccuping, and belching. Right from birth, though, you would do well to bathe the baby in speech at appropriate times. If you are overdoing it, the baby will simply switch off his attention.

You can tell him how much you love him, describe the steps by which you are caring for him, hold forth on the issues of the day, recite the Preamble to the Constitution or the Gettysburg Address, reminisce, ask his opinion of conditions in the stock market, sing songs, recite poetry, whatever. But verbalize, and *molto vivace*. My neighbors used to remark facetiously that they had enjoyed my rendering of "Old Man River" or "Beale Street Blues" or "Battle Hymn of the Republic," and I know I must have sounded an idiot (I do not count a singing voice among my assets), but I persevered in the later-justified conviction that I was raising linguistically able children. Many parents feel foolish or self-conscious talking to a baby who can neither understand nor answer back, but they owe it to the baby to do so. Once the baby has begun to smile, talking to him is a good way to get him to smile, which you will find is a powerful reinforcer that encourages you to go on talking. By age two months, the baby listens attentively, and writhes and wriggles and works his mouth in an effort to reply.

Stages in Learning to Talk

The baby's vocalization begins with babbling, at first a collection of repeated vowel sounds. Consonant sounds gradually emerge among the vowels, and by late infancy the baby is producing quite complicated sound patterns. It is interesting that babies in all linguistic settings babble at first in exactly the same way. By the end of infancy, though, babbling shows what is called phonetic drift, that is, it has begun to shape itself to the sound patterns of the language the baby hears spoken. The French baby's babbling takes on French intonations and cadences, the Japanese baby's Japanese, and so on around the world.

Babbling is an important prelude to speaking, but it cannot be thought of as a welter of sounds out of which language emerges. Once the baby starts speaking in words, he leaves off babbling. The baby's first words stand alone, though each word may in fact be a fusion of several words, as in "Whadda?" and the classic "Awgone." The baby speaks in one-word sentences, in which a single key term stands for the whole: I want go to "Out"; That is "Daddy" 's shoe; Pick me "Up."

Much attention has been given to the baby's first word, on the assumption that it would reveal something crucial about the baby's mental life. My examination of the evidence leads me to conclude that the baby's first word, when it can be identified with any certainty, tells us very little except that he has begun to talk. "Ma-ma" and "Da-da" occur in the babbling of all babies, and loving parents are likely to interpret these sounds as referring to themselves; closer observation shows, however, that addressing the parents as "Mama" and "Dada" may come rather late in the child's speaking. The same is true of many other babble sounds, which the baby may be using meaningfully, but then again may not. You can know for sure that the baby is using words only when he points to something and says its name, or a reasonable approximation thereof. What that something may be is almost anything.

Once the baby has mastered a few words, something akin to babbling is likely to reappear. It is as though the child tries to make a magical leap into complex speech. He talks in what is called expressive jargon, a flow of gibberish with some real words stuck into it. Expressive jargon, like skillfully executed double-talk, is very convincing, and the parent may think that it would really make sense if only the child would speak more slowly and distinctly. In fact, the occasional real word may give you a good idea of what the child is trying to convey.

Expressive jargon is not a very effective means of communication, however, and withers away, probably because it does not produce satisfying feedback. The child then settles down to piecing words together into sentences, at first two at a time, and then, gradually, in ever-longer strings. The baby's two-word sentences are likely to consist of a noun with some indicator of an action attached, as in "Baby, crying," or "Car, backing up." (The commas represent pauses indicating the laborious hooking together of words; in the second example, "backing up" is probably a single psychological unit.) The baby's early sentences get along without such standard parts of speech as articles, prepositions, conjunctions, and most qualifying adjectives and adverbs. There are no grammatical indicators of time and number. There are at first no words referring to the baby and his own states of being. He says "Eat" but not "Hungry," "Sleep" but not "Tired." Some fairly abstract words do crop up rather early: *more,* in the sense of "I want some more," not in the sense of "There are more people than chairs"; *back,* in the sense of "Back to where we came from" or "Back the way we came"; *again;* and *forget.*

A great deal of thought has been given to the question

of what motivates the child to learn to speak. My answer is very simple: speaking and being spoken to. Communication is an intrinsically gratifying human activity, and language enhances the possibilities for communicating. More fundamental, though, is a property of language that Jean Piaget dubbed verbal realism, or symbolic realism. This means that for the child, language is not merely a system of labels standing for aspects of reality; instead, language is an inherent part of reality, and linguistic events have all the reality of actual happenings in the world. Thus, to be able to speak gives one a magical power over reality, since in speaking we are creating a world.

We all learn, sooner or later, that we cannot act directly on physical reality with words—although sometimes we can with words get other people to act—but the magic never gets completely washed out. There are many residues of word realism in adults. Euphemism, or substituting innocuous words for emotionally disturbing ones, exposes the fact that words can be emotionally upsetting. The childhood chant about sticks and stones simply isn't true. You can do all kinds of things to people with well-chosen words. You can wound them, sicken them, infuriate them, soothe them, arouse them sexually, and move them to tears or laughter. It is word realism that permits what is variously called reification or hypostasis, the creation of purely verbal entities which are reacted to as though they actually exist: poltergeists, Santa Claus, the bugaboos with which government officials frighten us into submitting to new taxes. Finally, it is word realism that permits us to become emotionally involved in novels, plays, and similar works of the imagination.

If we can accept that words have their own psychological existence for adults, we can understand how they constitute a magical universe for the child. Even though we need no extrinsic explanation for the child's urge to speak, we do need to be aware of some contrary forces. If the child's speaking is too consistently ignored or rebuffed, the incentive to speak withers. Adults must learn to listen. And, as O.H. Mowrer has said, if the language addressed to the child is too unvaryingly hostile and abusive, as in frequent scoldings, the child will not develop an urge to speak.

The child learns words and, in addition, the largely unspoken rules by which words are combined into utterances to represent states of affairs. Notice that we use grammar and syntax long before we have any inkling that there is such a thing, and even when we learn about grammar, a lot gets left out and much of what we are taught is at best only partly correct. The most proficient speakers and writers operate more by intuition than by a formal code of usage. None of the usual psychological theories of learning gives an adequate account of how we acquire such guiding intuitions. Indeed, Noam Chomsky takes the radical stand that they are not acquired at all, but are wired into the human nervous system.

Just a small amount of observation of a child grappling with grammatical forms, however, should convince you that some kind of learning is going on. For instance, the child will learn correctly irregular forms, such as certain past tenses and plurals, but then as he begins to master the rules, he misapplies them. Thus, the child who has learned to say "I brought" will switch to "I bringed," "I brang" (perhaps by analogy to *ring, rang*) , "I branged," and even "I broughted." He goes from "foot" to "feet" to "foots" and "feets." He says, "I walk homed," and "He pick it ups." When he begins to ask questions, he prefaces a declarative statement with an interrogatory particle, as in "May I can have some?" or "Is it is a dog?" He expresses negation as abundantly as possible, as in "No, I don't not have none."

These errors are obviously intelligent errors, and underscore that the child does not learn by simple imitation, since it is obvious that the people around him do not use these forms. One of the wonders of language learning is that every normal child becomes able to say things he has never heard said; that is, he is learning a whole system which permits him to express his own ideas, and not merely parrot what other people tell him.

Both everyday observation and formal analyses tell us that people achieve vastly different levels of linguistic skill. One attempt to categorize these differences is Basil Bernstein's much debated distinction between restricted codes and elaborated codes. Restricted codes are styles of speaking which convey a minimum of information. Elaborated codes of speaking involve complex sentence structures, are rich in modifiers, and offer explanations as well as facts. Bernstein relates these different styles to social class, associating restricted codes with the lower classes and elaborated codes with the middle and upper classes. It turns out, however, that all social groups have different areas in which they use elaborated or restricted codes. It is important to realize that a child's capacity to learn is much greater than what you would infer from the things he says. This means that it is important to speak to him in elaborated codes, both to convey to him the richness of the world and to give him a good model for speaking.

Thus, even though the child learns only some of his language—and associated thought processes—through direct imitation of adults, it is the adults who provide him with more general models of linguistic styles. Very little direct instruction is involved. Parents occasionally correct children's errors, especially when the child mislabels something. Also, as Courtney Cazden and David McNeill have shown, when talking with the child, the parent may expand and elaborate on what the child says. For instance, the child says, "Doggie," and the parent replies, "Yes, that's a dog, but he won't bite." Children tend to be confused by the pronouns *I* and *you,* thinking that they are labels for particular people rather than designations that get switched around from speaker to speaker. When the child refers to himself as "you," I have found it helpful to ask him, "Can you say, 'I want to go out'?" Repeating the model sentence seems to give the child the general idea, and the problem goes away. In general, children learn simply by hearing people speak, and do a remarkably good job on their own.

As Piaget has pointed out, young children are egocentric in their view of the world, and assume that everybody else must perceive and interpret things exactly as they themselves do. Egocentricity shows up in the child's language in that he seems to take it for granted that you know what he wants to say on any topic, so all he has to do is give you a few hints. For this reason, many statements by children are unintelligible except with lengthy questioning. The child may think you woefully dense for not knowing right away what he is driving at, but this is a risk you have to take as you try to understand him. What is worse is to think you have understood the child when you haven't. Learning that other people have their own perspective, spatial viewpoint, knowledge, values, beliefs, and understandings, all of which may be very different from one's own but which have to be taken into account if communication is going to take place, is one of the most arduous lessons of growing up and is rarely completely mastered. Even if one can arrange to spend his life among those he considers "his own kind" he will still find many obstacles to communication. It helps in dealing with children to realize how egocentric they are, and it also helps if we can become conscious of how egocentric we ourselves may be.

Egocentric or not, the child wants to make himself understood and will work hard at it if encouraged. He is beginning the lifelong process of ordering his experience linguistically, making a verbal map of the universe so that he can understand it and think about it. In the early stages, he needs a responsive adult on whom to try out his ideas, just as we adults may seek out a friend as a sounding board when we want to think through some problem—or sometimes when we just want to find out how we really feel about something.

Not all of the child's speech is serious. If his models

use language playfully, if they play with sounds, words, and ideas, if they venture into imagination, he gets the idea from them and does likewise. When reading nursery rhymes to the child, it is important to follow the text precisely—any deviation will disturb the child. On the other hand, children are delighted when, in reciting (as opposed to reading) nursery rhymes, you invent variations such as "Little Miss Muffet sat in a corner, eating hot cross buns," or "along came a spider, sat down beside her, and asked if he could have some, too."

Edith Hunter has written a delightful book, *Conversations with Children,* telling about some of the playful themes explored by parents and chidren. Some of these are parental inventions, some come from the children. One game discovered by numerous children is "What if?"— there were only men in the world; our car fell in the lake; a wind came along and blew off all your clothes. There are endless possibilities, many of them dire.

Psychologists and linguists have analyzed children's language at a number of levels: sounds, vocabulary, grammar, and syntax. My own interest is in the logical use that children make of language, the semantic operations they perform, such as specifying similarities, drawing contrasts, defining words, counting and summing, drawing inferences, bragging, lying, making jokes, and asking different kinds of questions—about causes and motives and purposes, about origins, about how to do things. (A half-dozen mothers and fathers are currently collecting observations for me.)

Children, as we know, are full of cute sayings. These are a lot of fun, but they are more than that. They give us insights into the child's thought processes, which are often radically different from those of adults. For this reason, adult amusement is an insufficient response. You can take advantage of these glimpses into your child's thinking to better understand how he operates, and sometimes to correct specific misunderstandings or gaps in knowledge. If the child expresses animistic ideas, showing that he believes that clouds move of their own volition, or that trees have feelings, or that his playthings can talk, there is nothing much you can do about it. If, on the other hand, he thinks that he will change sex in the course of growing up (a far from uncommon belief), you can at least try telling him or her that this is not the case. There are characteristics of childish thinking which, like egocentrism, simply have to be outgrown slowly. Other characteristics may be modifiable, if you can get at the basic assumption and beliefs. Don't be disappointed, though, when the child's thinking seems impervious to your instruction. There are limits to your influence, and you have to live with that fact.

Baby Talk

As everybody knows, babies talk baby talk, which sometimes makes them hard to understand. Some parents talk their own version of baby talk right back at the baby. A certain amount of parental baby talk is probably inevitable, and may even be beneficial, but the rule is to give the baby sound linguistic models to learn from. On the other hand, don't be so appalled at the imperfections in the baby's speech that you set about immediately trying to set them right. This is unnecessary; the baby will in due course speak correctly, or at least as correctly as his models. But this zeal to "correct" the child's speech is more than unnecessary, it is potentially harmful. It holds the danger that it will make the child prematurely self-conscious about speaking, and hence reluctant to speak at all. Think how you would feel if, every time you said something, the person you were speaking to pointed out your errors and then asked you to repeat your utterance, this time correctly. The child expects people to respond to his ideas, not his pronunciation. Such faulty feedback may be a cause of stuttering, as we shall discuss.

Accents and Local Speech Patterns

Parents set great store by their children's speaking correctly, and wonder what they can do to ensure proper speech. Leaving aside the question of what constitutes correct speech (in Britain the B.B.C. sets the standard, whereas in the United States people seem to aspire to talk like an educated Bostonian), there are no special measures to be taken.

The child will speak in the manner of the people around him. At first, his speech takes on the intonations of the parents and others who take care of him. As he moves out into the world of playgrounds and schools, his speech patterns shift to those of his age-mates. During the school years, he learns the particular jargon of school-children, the "me 'n' him" locutions that persist through the generations, the "yeah" and "naah" and four-letter ornaments, and all the inescapable rest. He or she will be influenced over the years by actors and actresses, statesmen, sports figures, broadcasters, teachers, gangsters, anyone who provides a model for a possible life style.

A person's speech patterns are an intimate part of his identity, in part molded consciously but mostly shaped by influences of which he may be totally unaware. It follows, then, that parents should provide the best model they can for articulateness, and for the rest, trust to the fates. Whatever subculture their child ends up in will decide his ultimate style of speech. There is some problem for upwardly mobile young people—I have perfectly bright students at Brookyn College who may be severely disadvantaged by their Irish or black or Jewish Brooklyn ways of speaking, but I know of no way that this problem can be prevented or remedied except by the young person's own exertions.

Stuttering and Lack of Fluency

With the few exceptions I have mentioned, my advice is to leave your child's speech alone.

Parents become uneasy when they hear their child stutter, stammer, choke on a rush of words, produce garbled sounds or sentences, or in other ways depart from adult standards of fluency. As it happens, though, this is simply the way young children talk, and there is nothing to be done about it except to be patient. Indeed, I suspect that a large proportion of serious speech impairments are produced by excessive adult concern with how children speak. It makes perfectly good sense to suggest phrasings to the child when he is having trouble making himself understood, but it is potentially harmful to worry about his lack of fluency. Help him articulate his ideas, by all means, but leave his childish stutterings and such alone.

There are, of course, some cases of organic impairment, including defective hearing, which can impede normal speaking. Such physical problems should be detected in the course of routine medical examinations. They almost invariably have signs other than the child's way of speaking, and your physician can help you know when there is something organic to be concerned about.

Bilingualism

Many parents want their children to be proficient in a second language and ask about raising their children bilingually. This is not an easy question to deal with. Some parents bring up their children bilingually without thinking about it, and it seems to work just fine. That may be the secret: if you have to think about it or ask somebody's advice, don't do it.

If husband and wife have a second language in common, they will find it very useful for communications they do not wish to share with their child. Eventually, of course, the child is likely to begin to get the hang of the other language, and in fact will be on his way to bilingualism. But if Spanish or Greek or Hungarian or Italian is not your primary language, I would recommend against any arrangement seeking to inculcate it systematically. If English comes hard, by all means raise your child in your primary language; be secure that he will learn English from his peers. If, of course, you live in a community where English is not the standard tongue, you may have to wait for the child to go to school to learn English.

This brings us to a topic marginal to this book, but about which I feel strongly. It is my conviction that non-English-speaking children—who, for all practical purposes in many places in this country, means Spanish-speaking children—should be taught in their native tongue, with English taught as a second language. It is very easy to transfer learning to read in Spanish to reading in English, but it is extremely hard for a child who knows little English to learn to read it. Spanish arithmetic is exactly the same as English arithmetic, and once you can do calculations in one language, it is a simple matter to learn the corresponding labels in another language.

One of the important linguistic skills of Western society is reading. I am solidly opposed to formal programs for teaching three- and four-year-olds to read. But I strongly favor some activities that enable some children to read at an early age or that facilitate learning to read in school. One of these is abundant experience in drawing and painting. Cutting, pasting, and naming and matching forms is a help. Another is learning the letters of the alphabet, which is best done via the sing-song chant that most of us can recall from childhood. Most important, though, is reading to your child, which helps him grasp the important principle that marks on paper can convey meaning. Find interesting books to read, and read them with animation.

The language some people learn consists of stale formulas, platitudes, clichés, and irrelevant associations, and thus their language imprisons their thinking. But at its best, language liberates thinking and gives access to realms of knowledge, fantasy, and feelings which may far surpass anything we can experience at first hand. One of the most loving gifts you can give your child is freedom of language, a fluency and joy in expressing himself. You can also do your child and yourself a favor by keeping a written record of his most striking utterances. If you don't write them down, you'll forget them. If you do keep a record, your child will one day thank you for a means comparable to the family album of revisiting his past.

9.   INTELLECTUAL DEVELOPMENT

Both psychologists and non-psychologists tend to carve a person into components: id, ego, superego: emotions, motives, and cognition: innate and learned traits and all the rest. I hope it is obvious that all such partitionings are arbitrary and to some degree false. People may be inwardly divided, with their better impulses warring against their baser ones, or rational judgment struggling against irrational intuition, but these inner divisions rarely correspond to either formal or common-sense categories. You are thus put on notice: we shall be discussing an abstraction called intellect which does not exist. What we are really talking about is the child's congress with the environment and with himself, about how things appear to the child and what kind of sense they make for him, what he thinks about and how he thinks.

If we accept that what the child reacts to initially is the physiognomies and demand qualities of objects and situations, then we can understand that feelings are always an important ingredient of so-called intellectual functioning. It turns out, for instance, that many children fear being sucked down the bathtub drain. The parent may not even suspect this until one day the child announces, "I wouldn't fit, would I?" Indeed, a capacity for emotional involvement is at the very heart of intellectual development. In effect, intellectual development means translating emotional reactions into ideas, giving them shape and order and meaning. In the same way, intellectual development brings with it new capacities for feeling. At an advanced level, we can deal with the coolly rational, but even here we are usually guided by an aesthetic sense of fitness.

Language, as we know, plays an essential role in the processing of feelings into knowledge and ideas. The linguistically adept child maps the world with language. This is both good and bad. The good part is that when we internalize our experience through language it becomes a part of us that we can reason about and elaborate in thought. The bad part is the danger, merely hinted at in our discussion of verbal realism, that language can create a self-contained world, complete with unspoken beliefs and assumptions, that bears little relationship to the workings of reality. Children leap to many preposterous conclusions, generalizations, and judgments which seem to be dictated by their conceptual mapping of the world and certainly have little to do with their concrete experience. The child may enclose himself within an ivory tower of symbolic formulations compounded of wish, magic, ignorance, and fallacy, and never peer outside to check real life. The alert parent will begin from an early age to cultivate reality testing, the empirical temper by which modern man is supposed to question his assumptions and verify his ideas by reference to facts.

It is hard to foresee what particular nonsense your child will propound, but I predict confidently that he will spout it in abundance. One child concludes that peaches grow from the juice of other peaches. A child playing cowboy refuses to go swimming because "cowboys can't swim." Obviously, much will escape your notice, but if you spend a reasonable time being an involved parent, you will have ample occasion to correct specific misbeliefs and encourage reality testing. It will not always be easy, because children, like some adults, find their beliefs so comfortable, and contrary evidence so frightening, that they are impervious to cognitive change. Also, like many adults, children find it hard to tolerate ambiguity, to defer judgment until there is better evidence. They prefer comfortable error to nagging ambiguity. The typical child goes on believing in Santa Claus long after he "knows" there is no such person.

I am not talking here about the child's excursions into fantasy, make-believe, and humor, which are to be encouraged. Playing with the shape of reality through language is important both as a delightful pastime and as an exercise in imagination, abstract thinking, considering novel possibilities, and, in general, learning intellectual flexibility. The child learns in the first few years to distinguish between realms of playfulness and concrete fact. The way the child works at drawing the boundaries is shown by a four-year-old who had cut a boat shape from a piece of paper and asked, "Would this *really* float on *pretend* water?"

One aspect of the child's fantasy life that disturbs many parents is the appearance of imaginary companions. The child sometimes experiences his imaginary playmate with all the vividness of a hallucination. At other times, the companion is only a convenient fiction. How parents cope with an imaginary presence on the premises is in large part a matter of their own feelings. If they do not want to set a place at dinner for the phantom, or go to elaborate lengths to avoid sitting on him or kicking him, then they should simply announce that the child can make-believe to his heart's content but that they don't feel like joining his game. Most imaginary companions simply happen, are harmless, and require no special attention. An occasional one, however, seems to be filling a real need in the child's life, in which case parents should undertake to fill this need in a more direct way. For instance, if a child has an imaginary companion who is constantly scolding him, it may be that the child has an overdeveloped conscience. If so, he needs an extra ration of love and reassurance to make him feel good about himself.

Some Characteristics
of Children's Thinking

Until about fifteen years ago, American psychology, dominated by behaviorism and dedicated to abolishing all inner processes from scientific consideration, was hostile to the very idea of cognition, the study of knowing and thinking. Apart from a few experiments and some items on intelligence tests, very little was known about children's thinking. Now, of course, thanks to the attention belatedly given the work of Jean Piaget, we know a great deal about how children's thinking differs from that of adults.

We know, for instance, that the child's thinking tends to be highly concrete, tied to the dynamics of the momentary situation, and that abstract reasoning—which takes account of past and future, of hidden forces, general principles, and systematic organization—is a later development. Children from an early age take off on flights of abstract thinking, but they are liable to crash into left field. My friend L. J. Stone quotes a four-year-old: "When I grow up I'll be a man. Maybe when I grow down I'll be a puppy."

Children's thinking is dominated by egocentrism, which means neither selfishness nor preoccupation with self but that the child, when considering things other than himself, loses sight of his own existence and assumes that the world as given to him is the way things look to everybody. The child seems unaware that different perspectives in space, morality, or knowledge give different people very different views of what a situation looks like or means. Egocentrism sometimes comes out as selfishness, but it is possible to be egocentrically generous, as when the baby lovingly offers a parent a bit of this spit-sodden toast, or when a schoolboy buys his mother a pocket knife for her birthday. The toddler may so far forget his own existence that he fails to recognize that the reason he cannot pick up a piece of cardboard is that he is standing on it. One little girl, about three, one day pointed to her father's cheek and asked what that mark was. The father replied, "I don't know. Did I cut myself shaving?" Her response was, "Maybe. Here, you look," and used her father's nose to turn his head in the direction of the mark.

Heinz Werner, another pioneer in the study of development, emphasized the rigidity of children's thinking, their adherence to set ways of doing things, their inability to adapt flexibly to the changing demands of situations. For instance, the toddler who, in playing with something on top of a coffee table, has pushed it off the far side may vainly persist in reaching across the table to retrieve it, instead of going under or around the table to where the fallen plaything lies. Werner interpreted rigidity as a way of coping with the lability of the child's experience, the sense that things can change radically and capriciously, including his own identity. Stage magic doesn't impress young children, who live in a world where magic is commonplace. There is nothing much to be done about the child's lability and rigidity. They cure themselves as the child's world becomes more comprehensible, controllable, and stable.

So labile is the baby's experience that up to the age of about eight months, he acts as though an object which you hide before his eyes has simply gone out of existence. Many parents have tried the game of covering a toy for the baby to find, and then have been baffled that the baby doesn't look for it.

In later infancy, the baby greatly enjoys games of hide-the-toy. He likes to guess which of two fists conceals a small object: if you repeatedly hide the lure in the same hand, the baby quickly learns where to look. Then, if you switch hands, he will go on looking in the original hand even after he has learned that the rule has been changed. After a few trials, his looking in the original hand becomes a vestigial, ritual touching before he moves on to the correct one.

The older child assumes that when you change the spatial arrangement of something, you also change its quantity. Thus, a row of three buttons closely spaced does not look numerically equal to a row of three buttons widely spaced, nor does a horizontal array seem equal to a vertical one. When the child sees a ball of clay rolled out into a "snake" or some liquid poured into a container of a different shape, he concludes that the amount of clay or liquid has been changed.

Up to about age three, the child takes it for granted that metamorphosis is possible. I have already mentioned that the young child accepts the possibility of changing his sex. In the same way, it seems perfectly plausible that a dog may be transmuted into a cat, or a chicken into a rabbit. We have to remember that the child's experience is a blend of stability and transformations, and it takes him a long time to figure out the rules of what endures and what does not.

The child may react to a picture as though to a real object. The classical example (observable both in children and in Keith and Cathy Hayes' home-reared chimpanzee, Viki) is trying to hear the ticking of a pictured watch. Children likewise pet pictures of animals, sniff at pictured flowers, and try to pick up pictures and printed designs from the page. These observations support the idea that perception begins with solid objects in voluminous space, and not with learning to infer solidity from the flat images on the retinas. Later, you can see the operation of moral realism, the child acting as though principles of right and wrong are built into nature, like the laws of physics or chemistry. Wait till your child first catches you telling a fib to a visitor and screams at the top of his lungs, "You're telling a lie!"

The child has to learn to coordinate the information he receives through his various senses. He cannot at first, just by looking, tell whether something is soft or hard, heavy or light, brittle or pliable or rigid, what kind of sound it will make when struck, or how it will taste or smell. Such associations take a while to master. He comes to know from the sounds he hears what the sources are likely to be, and so on through all our complex experience of objects.

Another important characteristic of immature experience is phenomenalism, the fact that the child initially is content with things as they are given, without wondering about underlying structures. Thus, the child learns to work light switches, faucets, radio and television sets and record players, without any concern for how these marvels operate. The child takes it for granted that the people he sees on TV are actually in the set, or that the musicians are inside the radio or record player, and it is the beginning of wisdom when he begins to wonder how they got in there and to worry about how they will get out.

Piaget has traced the development of the child's thinking about how physical events are caused. At first, events need no explanation but are accounted for by some all-purpose energy with which the universe is teeming. The child's earliest attempts to explain causation lead him to translate this pervasive dynamism into humanlike forces that inhabit objects and give them feelings, purposes, and the power of autonomous action. This way of viewing the world is called animism. Ruth, one of the children described in *Three Babies,* gives several examples of animism at age twenty months: she reproaches the stove, "Burn, hurt Mommy"; she drops a bone and cries, "Fall down—poor bone"; she hugs tables and chairs, saying, "Love you." In an animistic world the stone rolls down the hillside because it has an urge to.

Later, while recognizing that some objects are inert, the child still assumes that they are set in motion by humanlike agents. A child notices the ground carpeted with pine needles and asks, "Why did they put these here?" Kornei Chukovsky quotes a child as asking why "they" put pits in cherries, apparently envisioning cherries as something that roll off an assembly line. It is only in an advanced stage of thinking that the child can accept the workings of wholly impersonal forces like gravity and magnetism, or that significant events can be the product of coincidence rather than design.

There is increasing evidence that children have great difficulty synthesizing separate experiences. In a classic experiment by Norman R. Maier, children learned a number of routes within a maze. It was not before age seven, though, that they began piecing together separate routes into an overall "mental map" of the maze. In general, children have trouble "seeing the connection."

I have emphasized some of the ways in which young children's thought processes are decidedly different from adults'. You can do very little specifically to accelerate the transition to mature ways of thinking. It takes a long, long time, and even when your child is ready to leave the nest you will have reservations about his or her intellectual adequacy. You will have to let go nevertheless. Meanwhile, you can provide a loving, stimulating, responsive environment full of opportunities to learn.

Playthings and Materials

Many parents are eager to know what sorts of playthings will contribute to their child's intellectual development. The answer is simple: almost anything. I must say, though, that many "educational" toys leave children cold. One little girl I know told her parents, as her fifth birthday was approaching, "I hope you're not going to buy me anything *educational*." Regular household furnishings—the furniture, drawers and their contents, discarded magazines, kitchen utensils—are the primary ingredients in the "hidden curriculum." Nor should we forget the parents as playmates, playthings, and mentors.

Regular toys are good, too. Many toys can be made as well as bought, and the homemade versions are often superior and always cheaper than those found in stores. For instance, very young babies like having a mobile suspended over their bassinet to look at, and parents can fashion quite interesting mobiles with everyday materials, such as cut-out colored paper, coat hangers, paper clips, sea shells, and Christmas tree ornaments. After a few months, the baby likes to have the equivalent of a cradle gym, with rings (embroidery hoops and wooden curtain rings are useful) and bars (lengths of dowel with the ends sanded) to set swaying and to grasp and tug at. These are most satisfying if they are suspended by springs and if activating them produces interesting sound effects, like the tinkling of a bell. A cloth doll suspended by elastic is also good. Rattles, of course, have delighted babies from ancient times. The general rule, past the age of a few months, is that the baby should be able to do something to or with the toy; he should be able to make things happen and produce feedback (and the toy should be large enough so he won't swallow it.)

Quite elaborate devices have been put on the market by which the baby, simply by touching a heat-sensitive switch, can produce video displays or taped music or his mother's voice, but I feel that these are a bit much, even for those who can afford them. Babies who have gained control of their hands like to play with cloth and paper, twisting it, crumpling it, tearing it, and chewing on it (avoid colors that may run). Once they can creep, babies love to climb in and out of cupboards and boxes. They like to put things in and take things out of containers. Once the baby has moved to the family tub, water play becomes a delightful pastime. To exploit his bath thoroughly, the baby needs washcloths and sponges, floating toys, and plastic cups. A word of warning: even though he is having such a good time, it is not safe to leave him untended in the tub; too many babies drown that way.

As the baby approaches toddlerhood, he will want props for his newly mobile style of life. He will enjoy learning to ride a tricycle, even though he tries at first to push with both feet at once and needs time to figure out the need for alternating thrusts. Another word of warning: keep an eye on his trike-riding so that he doesn't go into the street or get in the path of cars backing out of driveways. Most children need several tricycles, of increasing size, before they graduate to a two-wheeler, so try to get a hand-me-down or secondhand one in good working order. It is at this age, too, that the child likes to push a corn-popper ahead of him or tow a quacking duck at the end of a cord. He likes to transport his dolls in a coaster wagon, although he tries to push the wagon by its handle so that he can watch the dolls riding, whereas coaster wagons are made for pulling, not pushing.

Toddlers enjoy activity or gadget boards with cranks and gears, and doors with various kinds of latches opening on pictures or mirrors, or simply the world on the other side of the panel. One that I had built for research purposes included a socket for a fifteen-watt bulb operated by a length of string attached to a pull-chain switch, and a battery-powered doorbell operated by a push-button.

Toddlers dote on the kind of pounding board on which they hammer pegs through holes. They enjoy music and love having their own record player. It should be sturdy and simple, but not super-simple so that all the child has to do is shove a record into a slot. The record player should have an on-off switch, a volume control, and a tone arm for the child to manipulate. Toddlers like to dabble in water and sand and dust and dirt and mud, but they demand to be cleaned off thoroughly when they're through. They like to scribble with crayons or ballpoints or *dull* pencils; their scribbling should be done under supervision so that they don't mark up floor and walls and draperies and upholstery. Children take pleasure in mastering the trick of manipulating boxes and eggs that nest one within the next. The toddler enjoys working formboards, fitting graduated disks on a spindle, and stringing large wooden or plastic beads of various shapes and colors on a cord with a shoelace tip.

Preschool children run, climb, jump, and slide, but they also find pleasure in less vigorous activities. They make ingenious use of all sorts of raw materials. They can cut out paper shapes with blunt-nosed scissors. They invent uses for pipe cleaners, paper clips, rubber bands, cleaning tissues, paste, and anything that can be glued or stapled or wired to anything else (most preschool children cannot tie knots). They enjoy helping with the housework and can learn to cook simple dishes. They engage in ever more complicated dramatic play, alone or with age-mates, and begin to demand props, such as a cowboy hat or an Indian headdress, for their roles. They build with blocks and run toy cars, trucks, and airplanes through their constructions. Late in this age period, some inventive kids are staging skits based, sometimes satirically, on fairy tales or TV programs or commercials. (On a car trip with her family, a four-year-old proposed, "Let's play that family fun game, Divorce Hearing.") Those children who are adept at counting enjoy board games like Parcheesi; doing so, they cheat, fudge, and demand endless exceptions to the rules and chances to change their minds.

Around age three, the child begins to make pictorial representations, especially if he has free access to drawing materials. The child's first drawings are usually of humans, and it is fascinating to follow the evolution of his representations of people until he reaches age five or so. Thereafter, most people's drawings stop evolving. The child's first people consist of a crude circle with a few marks inside standing for facial features. By age five, the child who has been encouraged to draw—not in words, but by being kept supplied with materials—depicts whole people, with clothes and implements, standing in landscapes with trees and houses and sun and clouds; the people loom vastly larger than trees or houses. He may try to show people in action by giving them jagged contours.

A word of advice. Please don't ever ask a child about his drawing or painting, "What is it?" In the first place, it may not have been meant to *be* anything. Even if it was, if you are too stupid to recognize the tiger or airplane, you do not deserve to be told. What one says to the child is, "Tell me about your picture," which usually elicits a detailed account.

Choosing Toys

Relatives and friends can be counted on to shower your child with inappropriate toys. There is nothing you can do about this except feign enthusiastic gratitude; such gifts have been known to vanish mysteriously during the night. However, when you are doing the buying, you can be more savvy. One useful general rule is that the size of the toy should be roughly in inverse proportion to the size of the child. You don't give an infant or toddler tiny things, if only because he will put them in his mouth and is liable to swallow or choke on them.

Preschool children, by contrast, enjoy and can use miniature houses and figurines. I don't know that it really makes a great difference, but by all means let the child have an interracial assortment of dolls. (It does make a difference if he can have an interracial assortment of playmates.) Don't worry about sex-role appropriateness. Your son is not going to become a homosexual because he plays with dolls and doll furnishings, or your daughter because she builds with blocks and plays with trucks. And don't worry too much about aesthetics. If, other considerations being equal, you have a choice between toys that are more or less aesthetically pleasing, take the more pleasing model. But children have lousy taste and the search for aesthetic purity in playthings can lead to a sterile blandness.

By all means, avoid war toys. They themselves will not make your child a killer, but they help create an atmosphere in which military and violent solutions to social problems come to be taken for granted. At older ages, quasi-weapons like darts and bows and arrows and even slingshots with which to knock over tin cans can be fun, but these are much too dangerous for preschool children.

If your child's behavior doesn't tell you what is appropriate for his age, then let what I have said serve as a rough guide. There are some toys, such as balls and dolls and stuffed animals and pounding boards and stacking blocks and small wagons, that span a wide range and can be played with in ever more mature ways.

Assuming that the toy you have chosen is suited to the child, make sure that it is safe. If it is painted, make sure that the paint is lead-free. Small children suck and chew on their toys, and lead in their diet can be disastrous. Make sure that the toy doesn't have detachable small components that can go in the baby's mouth. Make sure it is free of splinters and potential splinters and slivers. Don't buy toys containing easily breakable glass. If the toy is made of plastic, be sure it is noncombustible, strong, and securely fastened at the joints. Don't buy toys or decorations made of seeds or nuts—some of these have turned out to be poisonous. I am not enough of an expert to advise you on fabrics and stuffing materials, but try to take account of flammability, allergies, and toxicity.

Finally, make sure that what you buy is durable. Babies and young children give their playthings a rough time, and all too many toys disintegrate rapidly. Some of them, indeed, never make it out of the box. Inspect the particular specimen you plan to buy while you are in the store, and reject it on any sign of flimsiness. Better to make your own, or let the child make do with what is around the house, than to waste money on playthings that will shatter, crack, shred, crumble, or malfunction in ordinary use.

Deprivation, Stimulation, and Overstimulation

It is often said that the child needs abundant stimulation to develop well intellectually. This is only partly so. What the child needs is adequate amounts of beneficial stimulation. Even the loving and well-loved parent can intrude on the child, lavishing affection when the child would rather be investigating a drawer or looking at himself in the mirror. The materials of stimulation should be available to the child, but he should have a large measure of control over when he chooses to be stimulated, and by what.

A number of observers have pointed out that it is inaccurate to describe the plight of poor children as psychological deprivation. Some poor children are indeed understimulated. They may lack many of the environmental ingredients for sound emotional and intellectual development, including the human stimulation that has come to be a standard feature of middle-class child rearing. But at the same time, many urban poor children are overstimulated: too many people in too little space, too much talk, coercive discipline, a television set pouring out endless sounds and images, a crowded bed that may be wet as often as it is dry, rats in and out of the woodwork, the smells of decay, too much heat or too much cold. And with it all, the child is expected to be inactive, unobtrusive, and undemanding.

There is a danger that parents—whether because of social conditions or out of harking to the motto of stimulation—will overwhelm their baby with more than he can take in, enjoy, and make sense of. The overstimulated baby learns to stop attending, to block out unwanted sights and sounds. This defense against chaos also works, unfortunately, to shut off beneficial stimulation.

Closely related is the tendency of some parents to try to force intellectual precocity. Parents who want their children to be bright have to understand the difference between giving a child abundant opportunities to learn and demanding that he master certain intellectual skills. Forcing, like overstimulation, simply makes the child switch off. At best, he loses whatever spontaneous interest he had in the activity; at worst, he develops a profound and perhaps permanent antipathy for it.

The Concept of Intelligence

Everybody knows intuitively what we mean by intelligence, the easily observable fact that there are wide individual differences in the adequacy with which people deal with problems that require knowledge and thought. Most people assume that these differences are organic, and when pressed, will say that they are related to variations in the structure and functioning of brains. Yet long years of scientific research have taught us precious little about what these variations may be. We have learned to identify a number of pathologies. Brains that depart markedly in size from the average, whether in the direction of bigness or smallness, are liable not to work as well as they should. Some brains show abnormal patterns of electrical discharge, sometimes in association with one form of epilepsy or another, sometimes not. Sometimes people are born with incomplete or incompletely developed brains; we are only beginning to appreciate that this may be true of vast numbers of people whose mothers' diets were deficient in protein. Some people have disordered endocrine glands, whose secretions have an unfavorable influence on growth and brain functioning. Some people have an abnormal set of chromosomes, sometimes hereditary in the usual sense but sometimes produced by the actions of X-rays or viruses on one of the ova stored in the mother's body, and in some cases—such as mongolism—brain development is abnormal.

While any of these conditions may affect intellectual

functioning, their influence is not as direct or as clearly defined as one might think. Some mongoloids are of normal intelligence, and one hears of an occasional mongoloid who is quite bright. Brain damage often brings with it some impairment of intellectual functioning, but not necessarily. The literature describes several patients who had the dominant hemisphere of the brain removed but who lived long enough to recover from the surgery and showed no detectable intellectual deficit. In any event, these brain pathologies collectively occur in no more than, at a generous estimate, ten or fifteen percent of the population. Any neurological variations which might account for intellectual differences in the normal eighty-five or ninety percent of the population are almost totally unknown. The little we know comes from experiments with animals demonstrating that brain structure and function can be modified by experiences in early life.

Thus, in spite of what some experts are prepared to tell us, we have very little solid knowledge about the biology of intellectual differences. Even if we know something about it, we still could not assert that biological variations are genetically determined, as those who talk about racial differences are inclined to do. We know too much about prenatal influences, particularly the mother's diet, to take it for granted that characteristics observable at birth were fixed by the actions of genes.

I do not want to get too deeply into matters of genetics. There are, however, two points that you might bear in mind in thinking about these matters. One is that complex human traits, such as intelligence, or schizophrenia, must of necessity involve a number of genes, and so-called polygenic traits are highly sensitive to environmental modification. (Eye color is determined by a single gene pair and is very hard to modify, but stature is a multi-gene trait and is very easy to modify, as we discover when we see third-generation Japanese-Americans towering over their grandparents.) The second point is that a gene does not carry a single fixed message but can find many different expressions depending on the context in which it does its work. What a baby inherits is not a fixed program of development but a flexible scheme with a great many developmental possibilities.

On the psychological side, our knowledge is not much more secure. Where many laymen and professionals go seriously astray in their thinking about intelligence is to consider it a one-dimensional trait on which people score high or low. Intelligence tests examine quite diverse sorts of abilities: defining words, general information, knowing social conventions, spotting logical absurdities, specifying similarities and differences, doing mental arithmetic, copying designs, putting a scrambled comic strip in the correct order, tracing a path through a paper-and-pencil maze, memorizing a brief story or a string of digits. Among the many sins of most test makers and users is that they add up or average the scores on these varied tasks, as though they were all measures of the same thing, to produce a single score, a Mental Age or an Intelligence Quotient, as a unitary statement of an individual's intellectual ability.

A different and less influential movement within the mental-testing profession has attempted to take account of the fact that very few people are equally developed in all kinds of abilities. A person can be high in verbal skills and low in mathematical ones, or low in both and high in his grasp of spatial relationships, or high in all of these and low in his ability to synthesize, and so on through a huge number of possible combinations. This school of thinking holds that one should provide separate measures of distinct abilities, called factors, so that the result of an intelligence test is a "profile" of scores on different factors. While this approach seems to make better sense than the one-dimensional one, the factor analysts have never made up their minds about how many factors are needed to describe the intellect. In practice, it turns out that the only limit on the number of possible factors is the ingenuity of the test maker.

My colleague L.J. Stone and I, in our book *Childhood and Adolescence,* have proposed a different way of looking at the matter. In our view, there is no such thing as intelligence, conceived of as any sort of entity. Without denying the important role of the central nervous system in behavior, we hold that anybody with a reasonably normal nervous system is capable of acting intelligently. How intelligently people behave is a function of how they conceptualize and perceive themselves and the world. Thus, what has been referred to as intelligence is a matter of relations between the self and the world. It is the world as perceived and thought about that differs from individual to individual—not their abilities. What resides in the organism is feelings, the capacity to use symbols to order the world and solve problems, the ability to put the present situation into past and future perspective, to defer action in favor of thought, and a sense of oneself as competent and of the world as manageable.

Instead of dissecting the intellect into factors, we prefer to organize the universe into domains, on the model provided by cultural anthropologists and linguists: into time, space, number, color, shape, causation, kinship, the supernatural, history and mythology, the self and all its subdomains, physics, physiology, music. Within any domain, we can define a developmental pattern of mastery in the facts, principles, and operations peculiar to that domain. It follows, then, that anybody who is interested in the workings of a domain can learn about it, at least up to the limits of current knowledge. One might have to learn something of neighboring domains, as a psychologist is supposed to know something of physiology and sociology. There might be several ways of entering a domain. In music, one might begin by learning to play an instrument, or by tracing the history of music, or by studying the principles of harmony, or by listening to representative works. Whether an individual could go beyond the present limits of understanding of a given domain would depend not on some fixed quantity of "intelligence" but on personal qualities of enthusiasm, drive, self-confidence, imagination, creativity, and openness to new possibilities. The last is especially important, since we are always in danger of getting locked into conventional ways of thinking. I do not know how to teach openness to new ideas, but I suspect that children learn it by observing their primary models—us.

10. INDIVIDUAL DIFFERENCES IN PERSONALITY

People mean different things when they talk about "personality." What I am concerned with here is individual uniqueness, the fact that no two people are ever exactly alike. Even identical twins, with their shared heredity, are always individually recognizable to those who know them well. To say that people differ from each other is, of course, not enough. We have to say something about the nature of the differences. There is considerable debate among psychologists about the best way to characterize personality in general and individual differences in particular. I am committed to a cognitive view, which says that the most useful way to talk about personality differences is in terms of different outlooks on the world, different ways of comprehending and valuing reality. Such a view involves a dual perspective: how the world exists in relation to me, and how I experience myself in relation to the world. In fact, it is easier to separate these two perspectives logically than psychologically, since the individual attuned to the outside world may be unconscious of his own private vision, while the person contemplating himself may have little notion of the extent to which his own existence is defined relative to the world.

Three things follow. First, we should be able to redefine personality "traits" in the language of self-world relations. Second, it is pointless to try to act directly on your child's personality. Third, what is good for your child's cognitive development is good for him as a person.

This last point has caused some people difficulty. The cultivation of intellect means the spread of a common understanding based on empirical observation and agreed-on rules of logic. The argument is made that as our agreement about world-views expands, individuality is diminished. I have two answers to this argument. In the first place, even if we could get perfect agreement on the nature of reality, there would still be enormous scope for individual differences in interests, concerns, and tastes. We can also count on the continued if lessened operation of human pettiness, selfishness, vanity, and so forth, even in the most highly humanized people. People are always arguing about the perfectibility of man, which is a false topic. What we have to be concerned with, in raising our children or setting social policy, is rather the *improvability* of man, about which there can be little doubt; the field of debate then shifts to the best ways to bring about improvements. The second answer to the accusation that I would destroy the very individuality I extol is that we obviously have to subordinate some of our individual proclivities to social conventions. People should be free to fantasize murdering the boss, but nobody's right to be himself includes the acting out of violent impulses. We do not want the grocer to use his own private system of arithmetic in calculating our bills; our system of doing arithmetic is not the only one possible, but it is the only acceptable one for everyday transactions.

Psychological uniqueness has its biological counterpart, although we can make very few connections between the two. It is obvious that having a very handsome body, or a very strong or healthy one, is likely to affect how other people treat us and how we view ourselves, but such relationships are not at the core of things. Everybody has his unique set of genes (here, of course, identical twins are an exception), with astronomical odds against anyone else ever having exactly the same combination. Prenatal events of the kind we have talked about interact with the genes to shape the baby's individuality even further. Each person's body tissues have a chemical composition somewhat different from everybody else's, so that his body rejects as alien any tissue introduced from the body of another.

What this seems to suggest is that even children growing up in very similar circumstances will take in and assimilate their experience in somewhat different ways, and even though sharing a general cultural outlook, will nevertheless be uniquely themselves. But even the assumption of highly similar circumstances has to be examined: Recent research has demonstrated what a lot of people already suspected: parental behavior is adapted to the general and specific characteristics of the particular child. Parents consistently handle boys and girls differently from birth on, and mothers in the nursery handle second-born babies differently from first-born. When we add on to this the specific properties of the baby as a stimulus to parental behavior—whether he is active or inert, responsive or seemingly indifferent, whole or flawed—we can see that parental behavior is not something determined only by what kind of persons the parents are, but is also a response to the kind of person they perceive the baby as being.

Even as parents more or less consciously mold the baby, they are being molded by him. When the process goes well, as Harriet Rheingold has said, the baby teaches his parents how to be parents: "Of men and women he makes fathers and mothers." Parents sometimes enter parenthood with strong preconceptions about what the parental role consists of, and about what their baby is going to be like. Sometimes these preconceptions prove to be unshakable, but more often, luckily, they disintegrate in the presence of a real baby.

As with intellect, some authorities place great weight on the biological component in personality, especially in regard to differences in temperament. Research in this area has not been of uniformly high quality, and you are advised to treat with great skepticism claims about stability of temperament from birth on. We almost always have to take account of parental practices. Margaret Mead attributes Balinese personality formation, tending to withdrawal, suspiciousness, emotional superficiality, and fantasies of all-devouring witch mothers, to the constant teasing to which Balinese children are subjected, and to the fact that social interchanges seem always to be broken off just short of completion or fruition.

Hans Selye has proposed that our reactions to stress are indicators and magical reinstatements of the techniques used to soothe us when we were babies. If our gastric juices flow when we are under stress, it may be because our parents used to give us food to quiet our crying. It would follow, according to anthropologist Morton Levine, that in those societies where the baby is soothed by having the genitals petted, stress should produce a sexual reaction; the hypothesis remains untested. William Caudill reports that Japanese and American middle-class child-rearing patterns produce differences of temperament visible from a few months of age. The Japanese perceive an active baby as unhappy, so when the baby becomes active the adult makes haste to soothe him. Americans, by contrast, see a quiet baby as unhappy, so if the baby remains inactive too long the adult stimulates him and stirs him up. As a result, Caudill says, Japanese babies are characteristically placid and American babies active. Nevertheless, it would be unsafe to conclude that these contrasting infantile experiences produce serene Japanese adults who are contemplative and restless American adults who prefer action to thought; such stereotypes cannot survive even a nodding acquaintance with Japanese and Americans.

We still have no very good way of accounting for variations in such traits as stubbornness, docility, adaptability, honesty, generosity, dominance, and introversion/extroversion—assuming that these are consistent traits, rather than reactions to situations, which has not been proved. However, since children strongly resemble their parents in these respects, it seems likely that we can fall back on the useful principle of modeling. Children become affectionate when they are treated affectionately. Chronic aggressiveness seems to be the simple product of a coercive, punitive upbringing. Violence begets violence, generation after generation. Those theorists who insist that aggression is an instinctive component in human nature often seem to me to be universalizing their own natures and projecting them onto the rest of humanity.

We do not, of course, become what we are all at once. We develop as personalities, and for some people development stops only at death. Whatever continuities and consistencies there may be, our encounters with people, places, situations, events, institutions, ideas, and ideologies have an impact on us and shape our outlooks. Nobody has ever adequately studied, for instance, the effects of growing up in very different kinds of physical settings: city versus country, seashore versus forests and mountains and prairie and desert, not to mention differences of climate. Anecdotal evidence suggests, though, that moving to a markedly different habitat can be very unsettling. The dweller in dense forest or jungle is said to be badly disoriented when introduced to the wide-open spaces. The Texan feels claustrophobic on a narrow, winding New England road. The city dweller feels threatened in natural surroundings, both because he is afraid of losing his way without street signs to guide him and because all sorts of dangerous creatures are waiting to pounce on him from their hiding places in the poisonous vegetation. Moreover, people form strong and possessive attachments to their native heaths and neighborhoods. Even slum dwellers forced out by "urban renewal" feel sentimental about the old block. It always comes as something of a shock to hear immigrants wax nostalgic about the homeland in which they were persecuted. All this is to indicate some of the still poorly understood complexities of human individuality.

I have made only limited progress in translating personality concepts into the vocabulary of cognition. But it seems likely that we can relate the all-too-common trait of anxiety to cognitive states of ambiguity and uncertainty. Paranoia can be described as a sense of great vulnerability to a world that is perceived as hostile. Values can be thought of as strong feelings of good or bad that are attached to various aspects of the real and imagined world. "Good" and "bad" are global terms, of course, and Chester Insko and I have demonstrated that they can refer to some five different dimensions of evaluation. A cognitive view of personality would have to talk not only about how our feelings and behavior are guided by knowledge but also about beliefs, convictions about reality which may or may not be accurate. We would also have to take account of opinions, beliefs which we ourselves recognize as possibly in error. Much work remains to be done, but the approach is promising enough for me to believe that the best way to give your child a sound personality is to give him a solid grasp of the workings of reality.

Personality Disturbances

Among the topics studied by students of personality is abnormal behavior. This book is about normal childhood, but some mention must be made of disturbances, if only to reassure parents that their own child is not in danger of going over the brink. Please be reminded that normal children think like schizophrenics, and that any adult who acted the way a three-year-old does would soon be on his way to the lockup or the booby hatch. As long as your child shows a diverse array of emotions, including love and laughter, as long as he can get involved in things and wants to communicate, his episodes of seeming psychosis need cause no alarm.

There are two main conceptual problems in talking about personality disturbances. First, except in cases of proven organic malfunction, there is, as Thomas Szasz keeps reminding us, no justification for speaking of "mental illness." "Mental illness" and its synonym "psychopathology" are simply metaphors. They describe reactions to life situations, not the characteristics of the disturbed individual. As Szasz says, the kind of life situation that produces the most profound disturbance is being shut up in a mental hospital.

More typical is the kind of family situation in which the child's behavior fails to receive sensible feedback, or contingent reinforcement. The child asks, "Can I have an ice cream cone?" and his father replies, "I see the Yankees are in last place again." Other families constantly put the child in what Gregory Bateson calls double-bind situations, where any course of action leads to trouble. Consider the Jewish mama joke: "Give your son two neckties. The first time he wears one of them, say, 'So you didn't like the other one.'" Yet another kind of disturbance-breeding situation is one in which the child's emotional and intellectual needs are not met, so that he fails to develop basic trust and autonomy early in life, and goes on indefinitely seeking satisfactions appropriate to babyhood. Note that I have said nothing here of traumatic events. What seem like devastating experiences, such as forcible rape or the loss of a parent, are traumatic exactly to the degree that the child has been made vulnerable by his early experience. The intact child, no matter what torments he suffers, can survive—with proper emotional support—some very serious psychological disruptions.

The second kind of conceptual problem we encounter in talking about abnormal behavior is saying what we mean by "normal." The common definition, on which I cannot improve, says that anyone free of gross signs of disturbance must be considered normal. In applying this definition to children, we have to remember what was said a moment ago, that what would seem abnormal in an adult may be perfectly normal in a child. Normal children give full rein to their emotions, they take very little account of past or future or the consequences of actions. They wreck their parents' sleep and belongings. They do not always distinguish between their fantasies and the real world, they hallucinate imaginary companions. They expect other people to meet all their major needs, they are totally stupid in matters of safety, they embarrass their parents by babbling family secrets, they are egocentric beyond belief. They cannot accept the idea of accident or coincidence, so that everything that happens is the product of somebody's benevolence or malevolence. If they weren't sometimes so lovable and amusing, we might be tempted to give them away. However trying we find our children's childishness, though, it is not symptomatic of derangement or depravity.

Although I am skeptical of theories that try to account for personality variations and disturbances exclusively in terms of organic causes, I must grant that organically caused mental retardation, whether genetic or caused by early physical disruption, obviously means that the child will have difficulty forming the kind of stable, coherent world-view that I have proposed as the mark of adult sanity. This is not to counsel giving up on organically handicapped children. They can learn a lot, probably more than even the most optimistic of us realizes. But such children need adult love and authority just as sound children do, and even if they are doomed never to figure out a new theory of the universe, they can still be loving, lovable people.

Where there is no demonstrable organic cause for retardation, be skeptical of such a diagnosis, especially in the early years. I am inclined to the radical position that all non-organic retardation is the product of inadequate or inappropriate emotional and cognitive stimulation early in life. What the child lacks is a sense of the world as attractive, accessible, and manageable, and of himself as competent. In other words, it is attitudes rather than abilities that matter.

This belief is not without supporting evidence. Numerous animal studies have contrasted the effects of raising rats or mice or monkeys in barren or enriched circumstances, with clear-cut consequences in the realms of emotional stability, problem-solving ability, sexual behavior, brain structure and function, and the endocrine glands' structure and function. A unique, remarkable study by Harold Skeels followed up two groups of people after thirty years. All had been studied first as babies in an institution, where they were thought to be retarded and hence unsuitable for adoption. Thirteen of these children were moved to an institution for retarded older girls and women where they were individually "adopted" by inmates, and incidentally by the attendants. The remaining twelve were simply left in the original institution. The thirteen who were moved received a great deal of love and individual attention. All grew up to lead normal lives in the community, most after a period of real adoption outside the institution. Of those who stayed behind in the original institution, no more than four led some semblance of normal adult lives. As I have said, this study is unique and is likely to remain so, but the results—Skeels gives a case-by-case account of the twenty-five individuals—are so striking that the lesson seems inescapable: early diagnosis of retardation is unreliable, and loving care, even if initially given by people of limited intellectual prowess, does wonders for babies. I have not proved the nonexistence of non-organic retardation, but I hope I have planted some seeds of skepticism.

For many of the same reasons, we should question the purported relationship between what is called "minimal brain damage" (MBD) and hyperkinesis, or overactivity, particularly in school, where the overactive child will not pay attention. MBD is brain damage which cannot be demonstrated by any of the usual neurological means, but is inferred from the fact of the child's hyperkinesis. I question the logic of postulating an unproven cause for behavior. I further question the logic of prescribing treatment for a hypothetical disorder. Large numbers of children—mostly boys—are being diagnosed as hyperkinetic due to MBD and treated with amphetamines, the family to which Benzedrine and Dexedrine, commonly called "speed," belong. Even granting that amphetamines help in some cases, I doubt the wisdom and morality of making speed freaks out of uncounted hyperactive children, in some cases contrary to the parents' wishes. I would take a stand that says that all normal children, especially boys, are in varying degrees hyperkinetic and that many schools are so deadly dull that they provoke their pupils to overactivity.

In my view, it is the children who sit still and swallow the garbage dispensed by all too many teachers who need attention. The standard school curriculum needs a radical overhaul. But even without such an overhaul, we could reduce the impact of hyperkinesis by making the classrooms a soft environment. There should be thick carpeting, soundproof, echo-free walls and ceiling, and the furnishings should be upholstered; the children should go about in stocking feet or felt slippers. What is further needed, if any reader is of an inventive turn of mind, is a window baffle that will screen out noise from the street and still permit air to circulate. Many city classrooms are acoustic nightmares, and it is little wonder that teachers and students are driven to the edge of frenzy.

It should be mentioned that a minute percentage of children show the bizarre symptoms of early childhood autism or childhood schizophrenia. There is a continuous and raucous debate on the genetic or environmental origins of these conditions, with the issue still in doubt. As in the case of intellectual differences, any genetic account will have to be a complex one. The pattern of inheritance would have to be through a multiplicity of genes, which means both that understanding the mechanism would be extremely difficult and that there is great leeway for the operation of environmental forces. Schizophrenia takes a great many forms, and there is some reason to doubt whether the category is any more useful than the label "psychosis." One problem with a theory of schizophrenia which views it as being built into the body's structures is that such a theory doesn't explain how it is that some schizophrenics recover and lead normal lives.

In fact, the difficulty with genetic theories of everything is that they invite fatalistic acceptance and passive resignation.

To repeat myself, the message of this chapter is to leave your child's personality alone. Concentrate on what you can do something about—love, play, playthings, talk, scope for the baby to try himself out, discipline—and his "personality" can take care of itself.

11. THE WORKING MOTHER

A few years ago, it would have been easy to write about the problems of the working mother. I could simply have taken a male chauvinist posture and said that women should remain at home until their children reach school age, when it becomes permissible to take a position that does not infringe on their domestic obligations. No more. Besides, all the evidence now indicates that having a working mother does no harm to school-age kids and may even be good for them.

Now, no matter what I say, I am caught between male chauvinism, on the right, and on the left, what Betty Friedan has identified as the new female chauvinism, whereby it becomes a sin to love one's husband and children. Let me say straight off that women have as much right to work as men, that all occupations should be open to everybody on the basis of competence, that men should share in the housework and care of children, not only because such sharing will ease the woman's burden but also because it can bring deep emotional gratifications for the father and his child.

This ideal of shared responsibility in homemaking is not easily attained. If both parents work full time, unless they do so on tandem shifts, which doesn't give them much time to be together, there is the problem of who is to look after the kids. If both work full time, they will return to a day's accumulation of housecleaning, bedmaking, dirty clothes, emotional crises, food to be bought and prepared and served and cleaned up after. The sex-typing of their early years has prepared most women for only a narrow range of occupations, and has disqualified most men for child care, cooking, sewing, and housekeeping. Thus, a new division of responsibilities requires that we redesign our sex roles, which may mean a shattering of present work patterns, habits of thought, and deeply ingrained attitudes. Frankly, I do not know how to solve these issues. Perhaps, though, a discussion of the problems will help clarify your and my thinking and point to some possible solutions.

To begin with, we have to acknowledge that not all mothers have permanent mates. Insofar as these mothers' offspring are unwanted, we may hope that improved knowledge about and availability of contraceptive devices —including that *post hoc* contraceptive, abortion—will diminish the problem. At all events, I certainly do not counsel chastity for unwed women.

There are widows and widowers and divorced people of both sexes who have children to raise, and there will always be a few women who want to have a child, either their own or an adopted one, without the bother of a man in the house. There may also be some men who think along these same lines, although I have not met any. Unless such a single person with a choice is independently wealthy, he or she should think the matter through most carefully.

The Mother's Decision to Work

Leaving aside for the moment all cultural and economic considerations, we begin with a woman who wants to have children and also to hold down a job. The first question to ask, then, is whether she really wants a child, and why. Working is not incompatible with motherhood, but the two roles conflict enough to oblige you to consider whether, in fact, you wouldn't rather choose between them.

If you are fully convinced that you do indeed want a child, then we have to raise the further question of how badly you want to get a job, and why. For some women it may be a matter of sheer necessity, with the only alternative living on relief, which, in its present form, most people find unsatisfactory. But one has to ask the realistic question whether, after paying for child care and help with the housework, there will be enough money left over to make working preferable to welfare. In any case, if a mother feels that she has no real alternative to working, she will simply have to make whatever arrangements she can and hope for the best.

Women who do not have to work may nevertheless want to. The possible motives are many. Some want the extra income to pay off debts or finance a few luxuries. Again, these mothers should consider whether the expenses of working, including the possibility that the family will land in a higher tax bracket, make good economic sense. Other women welcome work as an escape from the house. Obviously, some jobs involve far more deadly drudgery than any amount of boring domesticity, and the woman should make sure that she is not trading frying pan for fire. Other jobs, though, offer companionship, friendships, bowling teams, parties, flirtations, and, for all I know, affairs. Some women, of course, are committed to a particular career or kind of work. Such women may feel very frustrated, sensing the slow erosion of unused skills, if they cannot work. Some women want to work because it gives them independence, in either of two senses. Some want their "own" income, because it liberates them from reliance on the male or because it banishes a feeling of being a parasite, a quite unfounded feeling, we should note, since any reasonably conscientious wife more than earns whatever bounty her husband provides. The second sense in which a job confers independence is that it makes the woman feel safe in case she should ever have to be on her own.

Whatever the woman's motives, if she seeks a job out

of desire rather than necessity, she has to consider a couple of points. First, the younger the child, the more care and attention he needs. This raises the related problem of providing adequate, reliable substitute caretakers. These are hard to find, good ones are expensive, and there is the problem raised earlier, which I cannot emphasize enough, that it may turn out that the child you wanted so badly that you were willing to assume the double burden of motherhood and work becomes more the hired caretaker's child than yours.

The Trouble with Day Care

This is probably the moment to talk about day care as a way out for working mothers. Let me say first that the standard criticisms of day care are fallacious. The baby or small child in day care does not suffer maternal deprivation or estrangement.

The problems with day care are quite different. The best experimental day-care centers, such as those operated by Bettye Caldwell and by Mary Elizabeth Keister, have shown to everybody's satisfaction that babies can thrive in day care, in some cases doing better emotionally and intellectually than babies reared at home. Unfortunately, the conditions in university-based, government-financed, experimental day-care centers, which are supervised by skilled psychologists and educators and staffed by carefully trained workers, cannot easily be duplicated in your average neighborhood house or storefront. As soon as the ratio of children to child nurses rises much above 1:1, the sheer mechanics of baby and child care—changing diapers, bathing and mopping off, feeding, undressing for naps and dressing after naps, helping older babies with the toilet (including toilet training for toddlers), bundling up the kids to go outdoors, unbundling them again after they come back in—loom so large that there is little time for play and stimulation. Skilled day-care workers cannot be had for a song (if they could, you would become an exploiter), nor can the physical facilities needed for a sound operation—ample quarters, good climate control, the right kinds of bathrooms and kitchens, the right sorts of play equipment and toys, the necessary safety measures, access to outdoor play areas. Harassed and underpaid workers are not likely to be good for your child, and even capable workers cannot do much without adequate facilities.

Thus, if you are counting on a day-care center to play substitute mother while you work, please be aware that good day care is almost certain to be expensive. If you just want to put your child in a storage bin, then you decided wrong about having a child.

I have been talking so far about the working mother of a baby or young child within the framework of our present society. That framework cannot be changed easily, but it can be changed. It may come to be the norm, for instance, that both mothers and fathers work half time, leaving each a half working day for child care and housework, and still allowing the parents to have evenings together. Remember that we are talking about a division of the total amount of work to be done by a pair of young parents at a time of their lives when the child can contribute only minimally to easing the work load. This work includes whatever has to be done for survival, taking care of the dwelling, and raising the child. The conventional way has been to assign the first function to the male, and the other two to the female. Now we are talking about dividing all three functions two ways.

If you strive after perfect equity between husband and wife you are doomed; life punishes perfectionism with chaos. Take it for granted that there will be inequities, most of which will cancel each other out. Anyway, keeping score, even if you can figure out a way to do it, is too time-consuming; life is for living, not for checking up on. A corollary of this assertion is that you should avoid a mechanical parceling out of domestic chores: you make the beds this week, I'll do them next week; I'll do the cooking this week, and next week's your turn; etc. Try to make allowances for individual tastes and abilities. Some men are geniuses in the kitchen, but I am not one of them. Whenever my wife falls sick, the family goes on a starvation diet. I likewise make a botch of marketing. And I hate to make beds. On the other hand, I love babies and am willing to do more than my share of child rearing. I am an excellent cleaner of bathrooms and kitchens, and even find in these and certain other mindless chores a measure of occupational therapy. Thus, if it were necessary, I am sure that my wife and I could agree on a meaningful division of labor.

I have not spoken yet of the possibility of total role reversal, with the wife acting as breadwinner and the husband playing domestic, but it exists. If you and your mate can agree, and can tolerate the raised eyebrows of friends and neighbors, why not? I can assure you that the standard sex roles are decreed by culture and custom and not by biology. Pending the age of the test tube, the mother has to carry and give birth to the baby; if the parents want their baby to be breast-fed, only the mother or a wet nurse can do the job. But beyond these small biological restraints, there is nothing in her anatomy or physiology to keep a woman from being a hewer of wood, a tiller of the fields, an accountant, a subway motorwoman, an astronaut—or a jackhammer operator or riveter. By the same token, there is no biological barrier to a man's becoming adept at cooking, sewing, choosing the curtains, cleaning the baby's bottom, and maybe even making himself attractive and greeting his wife at the door with a sexy kiss and a well-iced martini.

Something resembling sex-role reversal is sometimes made necessary by a husband's chronic unemployment or physical disability, and I have no doubt that some couples find the arrangement wholly satisfactory. But this is not the same thing as assuming that one partner, because he or she uses home as a work base, as artist, writer, carpenter, plumber or whatever, is the logical one to look after the house and the baby. Home-based work, even if it is unremunerative or only occasionally remunerative, can be just as demanding as a full-time job, and constant interruptions can devastate needed concentration. As when both parents work full time outside the home, a third party must be found to care for the baby and help with the housework, and both parents have to pitch in to do what's left, including maintaining each one's special relationship with the child.

So far, I have been talking as though parents and child lived in effective isolation from the grandparents, which is the rule in our fragmented society. Sometimes, though, one or both sets of grandparents live nearby. In many cases, I have learned, the grandparents are a source of friction: they side with their own child against the mate; they criticize the parents' methods of child rearing; they actively interfere, overindulging the child or upsetting it with their own brand of discipline; or they become overinvolved, to the point where the parents feel that their privacy, autonomy, and integrity are being invaded. Sometimes, though, a congenial and cooperative grandparent can be the answer to the mother's working, especially if the grandparent can come to the baby instead of the other way around. A difficulty with this kind of arrangement is that the health and stamina of oldsters are less stable than the parents', and too frequent recourse to last-minute substitutes, such as dumping the baby in whatever day-care facilities happen to be available, can be unsettling for the child.

Once the child reaches preschool age, the parents have more options for day care. At least in the major urban centers, there are likely to be a number of excellent nursery schools. In the small towns and suburbs, parents can organize a cooperative. However, the nursery school is only a partial escape hatch. Entry to the best ones is highly competitive, and as you might expect, the best nursery schools can be formidably expensive.

Another important consideration is that most good nursery schools feel, with some justification, that a half-day program is the most that three- and four-year-olds can take and benefit from. Even when a school has an afternoon program, this is likely to mean an hour of nap time followed by half an hour of free play, with the children going home at two or two-thirty. Thus, even if you are ready to pay a large amount of money to have your child well looked after in nursery school, you will still have to find other caretakers for a part of the day.

Children of school age, as I have said, are likely to benefit from having a working mother. The child is in school a great part of the day, and when he comes home he can fend for himself, making a snack, doing homework, and playing in the neighborhood. During the school years, the child can take an increasing share in the actual running of the house. We are coming back to a realization that for many years middle-class childhood was a period of regal self-indulgence and overindulgence, which is not good preparation for life; we are rediscovering that giving children responsibilities that they can manage—and for all their seeming incompetence they can manage quite a few—benefits them. In the process of letting children share in the work of the house, you can help break sex-role stereotypes. Boys can help with the marketing, sewing, cooking, cleaning, and care of younger children. Girls can learn, from their mothers as well as their fathers, how to clean a spark plug or change a tire or adjust a carburetor, how to change a faucet washer or repair a light switch, or how to replace a bathroom tile. Although the working mother of a school-age child sees less of the child than the mother who stays at home, contacts between working mother and child are likely to be more intense and more satisfying.

One method of sharing the work which I can merely touch on is living in a commune. Here the housework and child care can be apportioned between two or more sets of adults. In the one commune whose inner workings I know something about, each couple has a tour of duty, usually a week, during which it assumes complete responsibility for domestic chores, including care of everybody's children. This does not mean that a child is isolated from his own parents; it means only that they have considerable freedom to come and go when off duty. But even the nicest people can be hard to live with in such intimacy if they fail to share certain important values, attitudes, and priorities. However foolishly or compulsively, I insist on having the kitchen counters immaculately cleaned after a meal; if I shared my kitchen with a couple indifferent to the state of the counters, I would find myself cleaning them even when off duty, meanwhile cursing the slobs who did not share my vision. In any case, I cannot speak for or against communes. They are not for me, but I am a product of another generation. Besides, nobody ever invited me to join one.

I fear that in emphasizing the difficulties in holding a job while being the mother of young children, I have given the impression that I am against women working. Nothing of the sort. But I feel it is important for husbands and wives to know what they are letting themselves in for, and to plan accordingly. Unless both partners can work part time, or one spouse is willing and able to put less time into his or her job and more into the home, the combination of parenthood and working inevitably means greatly increased labor for both.

Given present economics, it is probably better for the mother to defer working (or studying) full time at least for the first few years of her child's life. For example, some female physicians finish medical school, then stay home to have and rear their children for the first few years. They then go on to an internship and residency. Many doctors, male and female, have found it desirable to enter group practice, which, like the commune, permits sharing of work and scheduling of duty. Especially if husband and wife are in the same group, they can schedule their work so as to share responsibility for the children and also find time to be with each other. While this model is peculiar to medicine, it might be applicable to other professions. Obviously, the self-employed person is at an advantage.

It is to be hoped that employers in general will begin to be more flexible about both male and female employees who want to give more emphasis to family life, and less to earning money. To try out new life styles, employees need increased freedom to do their work at home, to set their own hours, and otherwise find means to earn a living without getting engulfed in their jobs.

12. A MISCELLANY

The Influence of Persons
Outside the Family

Parents are not the only people who have a say
in their child's development. For better or worse, lots of
other people intervene. I have already mentioned some
of the virtues and shortcomings of grandparents. I have
heard complaints from parents both about interfering or
critical grandparents and about grandparents who don't
do enough to help. For many parents, the neighbors—
even those they have never seen—are a constant presence because they can be upset by the baby's crying or
by parental shouting matches (most couples learn how
to shout in whispers) and they may judge, criticize,
gossip, and cast the young parents in the role of local
ghouls or laughingstocks. These paranoid fantasies are
not without foundation. Even when the neighbors are
at their most neighborly, bringing in a jar of quince preserve or offering to baby-sit, they may incidentally be
casing the joint, sizing up your affluence or penury,
sniffing out erotica, and looking for evidence of pot parties, orgies, and child neglect or abuse.

Parents also have friends, who interact with the baby
in ways that the parents find more or less congenial.
There are sitters and day-care personnel and doctors and
nurses, and casual strangers more than willing to shower
affection on the baby; there are uncles and aunts and
cousins ready with helpful advice; and eventually there

are teachers. In general, exposure to a variety of people and influences is good for the baby, and you have to tolerate all but the more distressing intrusions. You do not, on the other hand, have to give any great weight to other people's opinions—including mine—on the proper way to raise children. In the final analysis, it is your baby. You will know him better than anyone else possibly can, and if your intuitions run counter to the prevailing tides, you still have to follow them because that is the only way you can deal spontaneously with your child. No matter how much any one person knows about babies in general, each particular baby has his own ways that have to be adapted to by his parents. For instance, snuggling is something that most parents and babies enjoy. There are babies, though, who can tolerate just so much snuggling and then begin to resist it. Whatever it is that defines your baby's uniqueness, that is what you have to respond to. This is not to say that you should seek or listen to advice, but to point out that you should beware of anybody who seems to be trying, subtly or not so subtly, to dictate how you should relate to your own child.

The Problems of Older Parents

One father I talked to in anticipation of writing this book suggested, out of his own felt need, that I say something about the special problems of older first-time parents. I was and continue to be somewhat puzzled about his request, since neither he nor his wife strikes me as "older," and their little girl seems to me one of the Lord's chosen. I have, though, known parents whose first child came when the father was in his fifties and the mother in her mid-forties, and I am aware that certain problems exist. First, the decision to have a baby when the mother is approaching forty should be made in full awareness of the risks. The woman's curve of full fertility is like an inverted U, with its peak in the twenties. Young teen-age girls have a relatively high rate of spontaneous abortion and stillbirths. After age thirty, there is a slow but accelerating rise in the number of birth anomalies, mongolism being one of the more prominent ones. I have already mentioned that there are a number of contending theories about why this should be so, and I have stated my conviction that it is related to repeated exposure to unaccustomed viruses or to ionizing radiation, each such exposure increasing the chances that one or more ova may be affected. On the other hand, most babies born to women forty and over are normal, and the woman with a good health record may still feel that it is worth the gamble. Middle-aged parents should also bear in mind that by the time the child reaches maturity, the father may already have fallen to the grim reaper. Indeed, if there seems any great likelihood that either parent is going to be incapacitated for a considerable part of the child's childhood, this is reason for further soul-searching. Caring for babies and young children is hard, grueling work, and some older adults find their remaining stamina and patience under severe strain.

Newlywed middle-aged couples have an advantage over mates of long standing. Years of childlessness ordinarily mean that the couple has evolved a stable life style, including routines, habits, and casts of mind into which a baby may not fit easily. The newlyweds, by contrast, may be able to design their marriage from the outset around the expectation of having a child. Most childless older people that I have known have a distinct intolerance for the noisy, messy, intrusive ways of children. To them, even the best behaved tot appears a rowdy, undisciplined, spoiled brat. Typically, such parents seem to have little or no recollection of their own childhoods, or else conjure up a romantic idealization that would send their own parents into convulsions of incredulity. Sometimes, of course, the baby touches an unsuspected reservoir of feeling which, once tapped, gushes forth torrents of parental adaptability. Other parents, though, rigidly and relentlessly squeeze the child into the preexisting scheme of their life. This does not necessarily produce a neurotic child—babies can put up with a lot—but it may produce an oddly adult, unchildlike one. Such parents seem to like such children, but I myself prefer kids who are playful, imaginative, autonomous, and bursting with feelings. It is only parents who can unbend, frolic, and pour forth their own love who have such children, and, in the case of older parents, this may take some doing. Since older parents are, on the average, better-heeled than younger ones, they may be able to pay someone to help out, but I would urge them to turn over the housework to the paid help, and to keep the joys and pains of parenthood for themselves. Affluent parents must also beware of overloading the child with material goodies, and of a sense that because they have provided so well materially, his psychological needs must surely have been met.

Adopting a Child

Some people seem to think that if you can't have children of your own, it is a simple matter to shop around the adoption agencies for the right baby, take it home, and make it a part of the family. For some parents, it is indeed a simple matter. The baby triggers off the right sort of behavior, and the process of incorporation into the family goes along. With other parents, though, the magic doesn't happen so readily, and even when it does, the consequences may be unexpected. When the child being adopted is no longer a baby, other complications arise.

Research with both animals and humans suggests that the new mother's hormonal state, perhaps especially those endocrine processes involved in the fact that her breasts are giving or are about to give milk, helps sensitize her to the baby and respond appropriately to the signals he emits. No corresponding paternal state has been demonstrated, perhaps because it has not been studied, but enough men share empathically in the symptoms of pregnancy and the pains of labor to make it not far-fetched that they too are hormonally primed for parenthood. In animal studies, those females who have once borne a litter, even though they are no longer lactating, are far more likely to respond maternally to strange pups than are virgin females. This fact, together with my own observations, leads me to the hypothesis—and please remember that it is only that, not a verified solid fact—that adoption is most likely to take when the adoptive mother has already had a baby of her own. It is just possible that an adopted baby can reinstate in an experienced mother some of the hormonal components of actual motherhood, whereas the same psychosomatic response does not take place in the female without the experience of childbirth. If my hypothesis survives empirical test, it follows that adoption agencies should look for counseling techniques, perhaps even including practical experience in a delivery room or on a maternity ward, that would help women without experience compensate for the somatic differences between actual and adoptive mothers.

Even if adopted babies do not induce broodiness in inexperienced women, they do sometimes produce another psychosomatic effect. In my own experience, I have known several women who have been declared sterile but who, once they have adopted a child, suddenly find themselves fertile. I have heard of cases in which this led to serious psychological consequences. The first, adopted baby may find himself set aside in favor of the new, true offspring. It is as though the adopted baby, no matter how cherished, now seems an alien intruder beside the product of the parents' own flesh. The parents, sensing this, may guiltily try to compensate by lavishing attention and affection on the adopted baby, but forced signs of love may come out wrong and may be mistimed in terms of the baby's shifting needs.

It should be obvious that neither I nor anybody else knows enough about the psychology of adoption to offer any firm advice. I myself would like to encourage people to adopt babies (but with the warning that adopting older children is for the very dedicated, who can stand up to and endure the torments of a child who is likely to have problems of identification and who may be driven to constant tests of his adoptive parents' attachments). I favor adoption because in the first place, adoption may be an attractive alternative to adding children of one's own to an overburdened planet. The second reason is that very few foundling homes and their successor institutions can give babies the kind of individualized rearing that they need. Obviously, some very good people have emerged from institution rearing, but by and large the products of institutions are in various ways maimed. On the other hand, it is not a good idea to adopt a child in pursuit of some lofty social goal. Adoption is a personal, individual act out of which should grow bonds of intimate, emotion-laden attachment. It is all very well to say that you are going to rescue a child from the living death of an institution, but it is quite another to say that I will make him flesh of my flesh, so that even when I yell at him the yell is pregnant with love and concern.

Don't adopt a child because you think that it would be harmful for your own offspring to be an Only Child. Singletons fare at least as well psychologically as siblings. In fact, it may be the case that the undivided love and attention they get makes for superior development.

My message, then, is one of initial caution. Think it over and talk it over carefully. Examine your own motives. Expose yourself as much as possible to real babies if you haven't already had one of your own. This is especially important, since the abstractions may be so enticing and the reality so shattering. Then, if you decide that you want to do it, commit yourself utterly.

Traveling with a Baby or Small Child

It is an emerging part of our culture that young parents, on the model of an older society, are coming to take it for granted that they carry the baby with them wherever they go, whether on foot, or by bike, car, bus, train, or airplane. This is a healthy trend, far different from the anxiously elaborate ordeal that parents used to make of traveling with a baby. Babies seem to adapt quite readily; indeed, as long as they are in motion they tend to sleep. Even so, there are things that traveling parents should bear in mind.

Strange settings will not bother the baby too much if he has some familiar objects as points of reference. The parents, of course, are the key objects, and they should stay in touch with the baby until he gets his bearings in new surroundings. Bedtime, as I have said, is liable to be the hardest part, especially past age six months. Be sure to take along the baby's favorite bed toys and blanket. Let him fall asleep near the center of things, and if you move him in his sleep to another room, be sure to take his comfort devices with him.

If you are traveling by car, please observe safety rules. Select your baby harness or car seat with care; the kind that permits changes of position is desirable, but make sure that the baby is protected. If he is asleep in his car bed, anchor the bed and crisscross a couple of straps over the opening so that the baby cannot be thrown out.

If the baby has reached the age where he uses a potty chair or special toilet seat, take it along. As I said earlier, the young child may be unable to eliminate without his accustomed apparatus. Parents traveling with a young child always look like strays from a gypsy caravan, so you have to learn to ignore haughty looks in hotel lobbies.

Remember that travel almost always involves changes in the family's rhythms and routines. Do your best to avoid abrupt transitions—they are unavoidable when you cross several time zones by jet—and don't try to rush the baby into a new schedule. Make allowances for the fact that you yourselves may be made cross by travel, and take extra doses of patience for your child. If there are likely to be long waits, as at airports—and there are always long waits at airports—have playthings easily accessible to keep the child occupied. In restaurants, too, have things to keep the child busy while waiting for service. Move the sugar bowl and salt and pepper shakers out of his reach. In toddlerhood and the preschool years, the baby can amuse himself by unwrapping and consuming a few sugar cubes; in fact, it is a good idea to have something for the baby to nibble on so that his hunger pangs don't get the better of him. Mostly, babies are well behaved in restaurants, if only because there is so much new to see and hear and smell.

If you are going to visit friends or relatives whom the baby hasn't seen for a while, remember the facts of stranger anxiety. Don't casually entrust the baby to the arms of an unfamiliar person until he has time to get acquainted. If the baby is mobile and the new environment seems crammed with breakables, ask tactfully if you can move some of them out of the baby's reach. If your hosts are not wise in the ways of babies, they may feel that it is up to you to keep the child's grubby paws off their possessions, so be prepared for a certain amount of contempt. You do not, however, want to have to spend your visit perpetually on the alert to snatch precious objects away from the baby, or the baby away from precious objects.

Your doctor will advise you about problems of eating or drinking in alien climes. There are some localities where the water is perfectly safe for adults but holds the threat of diarrhea for babies. Remember that the foods your baby is used to may not be available everywhere, and you may have to carry provisions. Whether or not you use disposable diapers regularly, they are very convenient when traveling, and if you are going to use them while away from home, make sure you have an adequate supply. If you plan to use cloth diapers, think about how you will launder them. Not every corner of the world has laundromats, nor are laundry detergents always to be had. You may end up washing diapers with lye-rich soap, in which case do an extra-good job of rinsing them—and your hands. If you are going to a part of the world where medical care of the kind you're used to is not easily come by, your doctor may want to prescribe a traveling kit of essential remedies.

Community Resources

At home or abroad, you will want to know about facilities useful to you and your child. One thing that I have found out about urban parents of limited means is that they are liable to feel isolated, because they have little knowledge of the resources available to them. Some report that they learn only by accident of, say, a new play group or parents' discussion group that is forming. Some are unaware that they can get free medical care at the well-baby clinics run by the city or state health department. These clinics are operated primarily by public health nurses who—everywhere that I know about—are a special breed deserving the highest respect and affection.

I do not know how to go about improving the workings of the grapevine that will let parents know about facilities. Most mothers or fathers take their children to playgrounds in the parks, but a strange sense of urban reticence seems to keep people from getting to know each other well. It may be that such parents will simply have to learn to screw up their nerve and suggest to others that they get to know each other, that they form play groups or discussion groups or whatever, and start inviting each other into their homes. It seems that many young parents are still like adolescents, reluctant to admit their own feelings of inadequacy and apparently unmindful that others in similar circumstances share these same feelings. When mothers and fathers do get into a coöperative play group or a parents' discussion group, they find that it greatly relieves their sense of isolation. They also discover that there is wide diversity of thought and practice in the matter of how to raise children. Parents can do a good job of educating each other in this regard.

Even finding a baby-sitter may seem impossible. Again, parents shouldn't be afraid to ask. Call the nearest college and ask for their student employment service. Colleges may have rules about what time a student has to be in, and they may require that a student be escorted back to the dorm or returned by prepaid taxi, but such rules are not onerous. If, by some chance, the college doesn't have a clearing house for student help, ask how you go about posting a notice on a central bulletin board. Some dean usually has to give approval. College students make vastly better sitters than high-school students. I have eavesdropped on experienced high-school sitters, and it is clear that, in general, they are more interested in keeping the children out of their hair than in finding constructive activities for them. College students, by contrast, even if they have not had courses in psychology or education, and even if they are not yet thinking about having children themselves, are nevertheless likely to find children interesting creatures whose company they enjoy. Indeed, there is currently something of a cult of childhood among college students; I am not sure it is always rational, but for some reason they seem to like children.

In the city, of course, there are always entertainments for children. I take a dim view of most of the plays, puppet shows, and other spectacles designed for children. Even the circus is probably good for only one or two visits, and in large cities the circus is outrageously expensive. All in all, I recommend the simpler pleasures. Most cities have parks, and most parks are splendid places for kids and parents. An outing on a lake is an ecstatic experience for a preschool-age child (don't take younger ones, because they can't be trusted to stay in the boat); the child may at first find the rocking motion disquieting, but once he's gotten used to it, he is likely to find it enjoyable. Climbing on the rocks and picnicking in a patch of woods are likewise enjoyable. Children this age cannot launch a kite, but they may enjoy holding the string. Chasing birds or chickens has been a sport for toddlers and preschool children as far back as mankind remembers, and the birds don't seem to mind. The city zoo is a source of wonderment, but hold on to the child: I have just read of a three-year-old losing an arm to a lion, and a child's impulse to pet that lovable bundle of fur can have lethal consequences. The local natural history museum is an almost inexhaustible source of pleasure for children of preschool age and beyond. Small children don't have to understand everything they see; repeated visits over the years will bring an accumulation of insights.

By the same token, the glories of art are usually lost on young children, but your child may nevertheless enjoy a visit to the art museum. The first time I ever saw a Henry Moore sculpture, children were climbing in and on it, and I was depressed when a guard chased them away. The planetarium is only for older kids; the little ones are likely to be terrified. Any mode of travel can be attractive to children, and a bus ride to the end of the line may be an adventure for child and parent alike. As the child gets older, he and his parents can explore ever farther afield and in more detail.

The suburbs offer access to both city and country, and may actually contain some of both. There may even be one of the few surviving family farms nearby. Suburban life is lived by car, which tends to isolate the child from his surroundings. Try walking sometimes, even if the neighbors look askance. When you take the child into the city, go by train. Children have always loved train travel —and there may even be some faint hope of a renaissance for the railroads. Children enjoy a walking tour of the shopping center, which may have a playground with swings and slides and sandboxes and other children. Some enterprising shopping centers even have a trained caretaker to take charge of your child while you shop.

Religious Education

I have been asked on several occasions to talk to groups about how to transmit religious beliefs to children. I have tried to resist such invitations on two grounds. First, religion is the domain of theologians, not psychologists. Even when the invitation has been rephrased as the more general problem of communicating values to children, I have tried to point out that values are the business of theologians or philosophers. Second, I have pointed out the absurdity of turning for guidance on religious education not only to a psychologist, but to a psychologist who is a confirmed atheist.

In spite of such strong disclaimers, I have ended by being persuaded to talk, and what I have then tried to convey is quite simple. If you are firmly committed to a set of religious beliefs or values, then no special action is called for. You live according to your convictions, and the child will follow your example—modeling again. As the child begins to ask questions, you have only to answer them. And nobody needs a psychologist to tell him this.

As it happens, though, the assigned topic is often only a screen. Parents are not really asking me to tell them how to transmit beliefs and values to children. What they want to know is what they themselves should believe in and follow. This, of course, is a question that I cannot answer. People have to decide for themselves what to accept as the ultimate truth, or, if they conclude that there are no absolutes, they have to find their own ways of living with existential ambiguity. I am more than willing to set forth my own beliefs, but it would be presumptuous beyond saying to ask others to accept my gospel.

In Times of Disaster

As this is being written, large sections of the country have been visited by severe floods, reminding us that nature is not always a friend. Communities have to adjust every so often to the devastation brought about by floods, high winds, earthquakes, whatever. Research on the effects of disasters on children has produced three solid principles. First, keep the family together if at all possible. Communities used to have an impulse to move all the children to a safe place, leaving the adults to cope with the physical dangers and damage. This has been found to exacerbate the effects of the experience on children. They can tolerate a lot more in the company of their families than among strangers. Second, let the child help as much as he or she can. Children given an active role in coping with the emergency fare much better than those who are passive bystanders. Third, don't be afraid to talk with the child about what has happened. Events shrouded in an ominous silence are far more disturbing to children than even some ghastly facts discussed freely. A fourth principle is that those children who are not directly injured by a disaster may—like many adults—glory in the experience as a dramatic change from humdrum ordinary existence. So don't take it for granted that your child will share your sense of tragedy. For him it may be a gigantic lark.

Finding Professional Help

In general, the main link between you and various sorts of specialized professionals will be your pediatrician or family doctor. You should choose your physician with care. Listen to the scuttlebutt but don't take it at face value. It takes time and a few sicknesses to form an opinion of your doctor's professional competence, so your first judgment has to be of how good a personal relationship you can form. Does he seem interested in getting to know you? Will he take time to listen? Does he have the right touch with children? Does he keep his patients waiting endless hours in a waiting room packed with squalling kids and harried adults? Will he make house calls, or at least explain why this particular house call seems unnecessary? If he has too heavy a load of patients, is it because he honestly believes that he offers the best care around or is it because he is out to make as much money as fast as he can? Don't be afraid to use your intuition.

Public clinics are sometimes very good, rarely very bad, except for crowding. If you hit upon a bad one, change to another. If there is no other, get together with other dissatisfied mothers and descend on the local authorities. Let your newspaper know that you're unhappy. Fortunately, most clinics are staffed by excellent public-health nurses and by dedicated doctors, many of whom serve on a voluntary basis. Like other people who go to clinics, you will form your own shrewd judgments of which clinic personnel you relate to best, and you can learn to time your visits according to who is on duty.

If you have no one to refer you to specialized services, your best bet is to turn to a teaching hospital. Most such hospitals offer low-cost, high-quality services as part of their training programs for medical students, interns, and residents in various specialties. If they cannot help you, they will probably know where you should go. And there is always the grapevine.

For more purely psychological services—but only as a last resort—the best place to turn to is often the psychology department of a nearby college or university (some graduate programs in clinical psychology are located in medical schools). They may have a clinic of their own, and if not, they can usually supply the names of clinics or private practitioners.

But let me add a word of caution: psychological intervention in your child's development should not be undertaken lightly. Family life is complicated enough without involving one more expert in the intimate details. Most children survive the vicissitudes of being a child with less than perfect parents, and the chances are that yours will, too. No matter how thoroughly convinced you are that your child is on his way to growing up into some sort of maniac, give the crisis time to subside before you invoke the psychologist. Remember that a psychologist doesn't stop with the child; he wants to know all about the parents, too, and you should consider how willing you are to expose yourselves to his scrutiny.

A great many parent or citizen groups have been organized to help families with children suffering from particular disabilities. Some of the better known of these are the United Cerebral Palsy Associations, the National Association for Retarded Children, the National Epilepsy League, the National Society for Crippled Children and Adults, the American Foundation for the Blind, the American Speech and Hearing Association, and the National Organization for Mentally Ill Children, not to mention organizations for cancer, leukemia, and muscular dystrophy (many of these have their counterparts in other countries). Branch offices of these associations are listed in the classified section of the telephone directory under Associations or Social Service Organizations. The national headquarters of any of these organizations, located for the most part in New York or Washington, can direct you to the nearest sources of help. I most sincerely hope you will not need any.

Have faith in your love and your strength, have faith in your child, and may all your prophecies fulfill themselves.

INDEX

A

Abnormal behavior, 207-12

Abstract and concrete thinking, 185

Adler, Alfred, 26, 73

Adoption, 229-31

Adoption-induced fertility, 230

Aggression, 56, 119-20

Amphetamines, 211

Animism, 188

Associative play, 70

Autism, early childhood, 211-12

Autonomy, 125-27

B

Babbling, 168-70

Baby-sitters, *see* Caretakers

Baby talk, 176

Bad Seed, the, belief in, 20-21

Balinese, 205

Basic trust and mistrust, 59, 109-10

Barber, fear of, 45

Bateson, Gregory, 208

Bed toys, *see* Security blanket

Bedtime, evening, 78-80; when traveling, 232

Bernstein, Basil, 173

Bilingualism, 178-80

Biological clocks, 76-77

Birth theories, 161

Birthmarks, 17

Bladder control: waking, 101; sleeping, 101-02; failure of, 102-03

Blindness, 18

Body awareness, 155-58

Bowel control, 99-101

Brain damage, disturbances, 196-97; *see also* Minimal brain damage

ABOUT THE AUTHOR

JOSEPH CHURCH is a professor of psychology at Brooklyn College, City University of New York, where he has been on the staff since 1965; from 1954 to 1965 he was a member of the Department of Child Study at Vassar College. He has lectured extensively at other universities, has practiced clinical psychology privately and has done research on infancy, language development, the effects of social deprivation and on cultural differences in values. His other published works include *Childhood and Adolescence* (with L.J. Stone), *Language and the Discovery of Reality* and *Three Babies* (editor).

Before turning to academic life, Professor Church was an artist who supported himself by working as a railroadman and, later, by free-lance writing. Although he never lost his interest in art, painting eventually gave way to the fascination of studying human psychological development. Professor Church now lives with his wife and two children in New York City.

GET
HEALTHY!